Leaving

Adversity Plaza

Best wishes –
Kathy Ba

Leaving Adversity Plaza

You *don't* have to *stay* there !

Kathy Baker

To order additional copies of this book, contact:
Xlibris Corporation
1-888-795-4274
www.Xlibris.com
Orders@Xlibris.com
19963

Contents

Acknowledgements 11

Introduction: Welcome to Adversity Plaza 15

First Stop: *Bittersweet Boutique*

The Old Gray Mare 21

A Winter Story 25

Goodbyes 28

A Dog Tale 31

Irish Blessing 34

What's Your Season? 37

Up and At 'Em When You're Down and Out 40

This One's for You, Mom 43

Second Stop: *The Gallery of Shattered Dreams*

Change 49

Driving Blind 52

Lilacs: To Have and To Hold 54

Diaper Rash 56

Healing Ocean Breezes 59

The Pearl of Great Price 61

See Ya, Gene 64

Third Stop: *The Lemonade Stand*

"Don't Forget Vince!" 71
Rosalie's Christmas 73
Iron Bro 76
Fly Me to the Moon 79
A Little Bit of Heaven 81
An "Almost Oprah" Experience 82
A Tribute to Ann Landers 85

Fourth Stop: *Laugh Tracks*

A Big Fat Italian Funeral 91
"He Just Won't Die!" 94
Find the Humor In Everything 96
Try a Little "Tweeziness" 100
Lighten Up! 103
Coffins, Wrinkles and Integrity 106
Send the Grinch Back to Whoville 109
Free Ocean Vacation 113

Fifth Stop: *The Little Chapel at the Plaza*

Daddy's Tree 117
Angels of the Universe 120
Renaissance 124
A Child Shall Lead Them 125
Could It Be Magic? 128
Helping Hands 131
An Attitude of Gratitude 134

Sixth Stop: *The Wall of Mirrors*

What Makes Your Heart Sing? 139
Nothing to Fear But Fear Itself 142
The Carrot Philosophy 146
Life Lessons from the Velveteen Rabbit 149
Simplicity 152
Traveling Light 155
The Young Black Filly 158

Conclusion: Cinnamon City 161
Epilogue: Leaving Adversity Plaza 163
About the Author 165

Dedication

I dedicate this book, with love and gratitude
to my children,
Jay Kline, Mike Kline, Kerry Kline and Andrew Baker,
who are the most precious treasures of my heart;
to my husband, Phil,
whose courage in facing cancer and constant support of my writing
were the earliest inspirations for this book;
to my sister, Terry, and my brother, Brian,
who have shared my life's journey almost from the beginning;
to my dear "adopted" Baker family;
to all those whose examples of grace under fire
have taught me much about how to leave Adversity Plaza;
to God, who illuminates my life with love, abundance and joy;
and in memory of
my brother-in-law, Kenneth Eugene Baker, Jr.
and
my beloved mother, Catherine Amicon Burdick

Acknowledgements

There are many people in my life who helped in myriad ways to bring this book to fruition. Though I cannot list each one, I am filled with gratitude for every single contribution, large or small. Maybe you gave me one word that resonated with me and brought forth a story, or maybe you read my *Record-Courier* column and took time to tell me that it moved you or brightened your day. Perhaps you were one of the kind souls who kept saying, "I can't wait to see your book," and by so doing helped me to persevere in finishing it. Perhaps your example helped me to embrace life more fully, to laugh more, to take risks . . . to leave Adversity Plaza. Whoever you may be, whether our paths crossed only once or many times, I thank you for your gift to me.

More specifically, I thank my husband, Phil, and my children, Jay, Mike, Kerry and Andrew, who offered me endless encouragement throughout the process of writing this book, and cheerfully endured all the angst, annoyances and hand-wringing that accompanied it. I also thank my entire extended family, including my sister, Terry, my brother, Brian, all my Baker in-laws and my kids' "significant others," Lois, Belinda and Matt, for their support.

Shirl Matz and Rani Cargo, two heaven-sent friends, deserve special mention. Both of them popped into my life several years ago, just when I needed a new perspective. Each of them held up a "mirror" for me. In Rani's I saw my intrinsic value, beyond roles and responsibilities; and saw that I have a right to thrive, not just survive. In Shirl's mirror I saw encouragement to unearth my long-buried playfulness, and discovered a joyous, "I'm not *quite* over the hill" spirit. Their encouragement helped my authentic self to blossom. Without their support, this book might never have seen the light of day.

I have been blessed with interest and support from many other beloved friends, wonderful business associates and clients, and the openhearted faith community at Unity Chapel of Light. I thank you, each and every one.

Sometimes having just one person who believes in our talent, who sees our potential, can give us the courage to spread our wings and fly. Over the years, this butterfly has been fortunate to have the help of several such people. I owe tremendous gratitude to John Dvorak, my long-time friend, former employer and first business mentor. Without John's constant encouragement (and early financial investment in my company), I may never have come this far. Thanks so much, JD.

I also wholeheartedly thank Pat McKay, my friend, rainmaker and mentor; Kitty Musholt, who coaxes butterflies out of cocoons; and Norma Rist, mentor extraordinaire, who taught me much of what I know about business, via her Boardroom Groups—a support organization for women business owners. And thanks to all those wonderfully talented and dedicated Boardroom Group members, who are my friends, mentors and associates. You're awesome, girls!

I am very appreciative of the kindness of Roger J. DiPaolo, editor of the *Record-Courier*, who gave me the opportunity to realize my dream of having a newspaper column. Thanks also to my friend, Judy Casey, publisher of *Focus;* Don "No Relation" Baker, publisher of *Akron Business Magazine;* and Stephanie Hollender of Fitness Quest, all of whom gave me early opportunities to see my work in print.

Heartfelt thanks also to Kathy Wise, whose contacts and encouragement resulted in two of my earliest essays being published; and to Kathy Lamancusa, author of the books in which they appeared. The doors opened by both Kathys gave me the first glimpse of myself as a future author.

Last but not least, several people who made direct contributions to this book deserve recognition. First, two talented writers who also happen to be wonderful friends: Katina Z. Jones and Bonnie Hilliard. Katina's invaluable editorial help, resources, publishing savvy, creativity and patient handholding (for years on end) were key supports that brought me, at last, to the finish line. Bonnie's marketing ideas, friendship and editorial expertise (especially "show, don't tell") were incredibly helpful.

A special, big-as-the-sky thanks to my friend, Cecilia Sveda, for her patience and talent in interpreting my book's message and creating the beautiful artwork for the cover.

I thank my friend, Dorie McCubbrey, for her words of wisdom, and for opening the door to LeAnn Thieman, co-author of the best-selling book, *Chicken Soup for the Nurse's Soul*. LeAnn, a BIG thanks to you for so generously providing the one and only endorsement I desired for the back of this book.

An exuberant bear hug to my son, Andrew, now eleven, who, at about 5 years of age, inadvertently gave me the title of this book. We were driving by a local shopping center, University Plaza, and he said, "Mom, is that Adversity Plaza?" The boy is a genius.

Thanks to everyone at Xlibris, a most wonderful, professional group, who supported this book every step of the way and did a fine job of producing it.

And though no human words can adequately express my gratitude, I thank my Creator, the inspiration and guide for every word in this book, whose message to me was, "Have faith, and I will light the way." I did, and you did. Thank you, Dear One.

Introduction

Welcome to Adversity Plaza

"You have to get out here."

Though I protest, the taxi driver insists that I must get out of his cab, here, now. As I do so, I look around and see only desolation— dirty windows, boarded-up storefronts, an empty, weed-infested parking lot. There are people nearby, but they seem lifeless, robotic. They walk slowly, as if lead weights are attached to their feet. They seem cold, as though all warmth, all comfort, all love, had long ago moved out of their lives, without leaving a forwarding address.

In panic, I turn back toward the taxi to beg the driver to take me to a better, safer place. But the cab has already disappeared into the darkness. Why have I been dumped here? What has happened to my real life, the one where I was in charge, the one in which I decided what to do and when to do it? The one where I had options, made decisions and things turned out ok? I was there, just a moment ago, but suddenly I'm somewhere else. Now, according to the battered, dusty sign overhead, I am in a place called "Adversity Plaza."

*　　*　　*

Have you ever been dropped off, against your will, at Adversity Plaza? The taxi skids to a stop, the door opens, and suddenly you've arrived at an unknown destination, a place you never expected to be. It happens to everyone, sooner or later. We find ourselves facing a set of circumstances we didn't choose—a lost job, a betrayal, a divorce, money problems, an illness, a death.

Whatever the situation may be, the taxi has dumped us off at Adversity Plaza. We stand there, feeling more alone than we've ever felt before. None of the landmarks is familiar. We are dumbfounded, speechless with shock. And we don't know how we will ever find the way back home again.

Not to worry. Repeat after me: *Everyone **visits** Adversity Plaza, but no one has to **stay** there.* You can hail the taxi and get out of there anytime, no matter what your circumstances.

Hard to believe? It's true. Everyone faces difficulties in life, but we don't have to relinquish all control. We always have choices, even if they seem very small in comparison to the painful circumstances we face.

The truth is, our lives are not determined by what happens to us, but by how we *react* to what happens. Have you ever noticed that some people who suffer tremendous losses somehow seem to experience tremendous joy, too? Consider Rose Fitzgerald Kennedy who, in her long life, endured countless losses, including the deaths of four of her children. And what of Anne Frank, the teenager who wrote eloquently of life's joys, as well as its sorrows, while anticipating her own death at the hands of the Nazis? And then there is Job in the Bible, who suffered terrible losses but still ended up praising God; and the indomitable Nelson Mandela, who remained a man of peace and forgiveness, even after many years of hardships and imprisonment.

Luckily, most of us have far less adversity in our lives. Even so, Adversity Plaza is full of people who are there only because they don't know they can leave. These people are victims of something far worse than whatever difficulties they're facing; they are imprisoned by their own beliefs. Beliefs that tell them they cannot leave this cold, empty destination. Beliefs whispering that they're no longer in charge of their own lives. Beliefs that tell them someone else has the keys to the taxi, someone else is in the driver's seat—someone who has decreed that they can't have their lives back. And so, they adjust, somehow. They trick themselves into believing, "It's not so bad here," and they surrender their lives. They unpack their bags and settle in at Adversity Plaza, resigned to the belief that "this is just the way life is."

But you *don't* have to accept adversity as a way of life. Let's go for a metaphorical walk around Adversity Plaza, you and I. As you read the stories about cancer and laughter, victory and loss, frustration and joy, dramatic moments and routine happenings, as you wipe off the windows and peek into the dusty, empty Plaza shops, it is my hope that this journey will arm you for whatever your life may hold. I hope that you will be refreshed, revitalized and filled with excitement about your own life, that you will see that help is always at hand, that you're never alone. In the end, you will realize that, no matter what happens, you can hail a taxi and leave Adversity Plaza . . . whenever you wish!

*   *   *

First Stop:

Bittersweet Boutique

Our first stop is Bittersweet Boutique. If you peek inside the window, you'll be able to see a bit of yesterday's glory in the faded elegance of this little store. You can almost hear the laughter that once lived here. You notice the charm—tarnished by time and troubles—that somehow still graces the clothes and accessories inside the boutique. You may not feel entirely comfortable here, but you begin to sense the ebb and flow of life. It's just like the fashions in this window. Styles change, life changes. And somehow, it's okay.

The Old Gray Mare

Some people are able to recall their dreams, often in vivid detail. I seldom even recall that I've had a dream, much less remember details. However, what I experience instead is lovely, detailed daydreams. Images come to me, unbidden, often while I'm driving or listening to music or praying. The scene in the image usually replays in my mind a number of times over several months, perhaps so that I will have time to discern its message. I believe that such daydreams, like "night dreams," have meaning for our lives.

I had a recurring daydream several years ago that you might find interesting. It starred a horse, an old gray mare; one that had seen better days. Then again, maybe her days had all been like this one—difficult, filled with effort—because it was obvious from her downtrodden attitude, her dull coat and matted mane, that her life had been no bed of roses. She was in harness, pulling some sort of heavy load. She worked industriously, straining forward, plodding along endlessly, showing no sign of rebellion about her lot in life. Far from shying away from her task, she barely even looked up when more weight was added to her burden.

Running through my mind like a video, constantly rewinding and replaying, the image stayed with me for quite some time. The details never changed; it was always the same horse and the exact same scene. What did it mean? Why did it keep returning?

Eventually, to my chagrin, it hit me: that old gray mare was . . .

me! As the gray horse's now-familiar story continued to play through my mind like a movie on a screen, I recognized that, for quite some time, I'd been feeling that my life bore an eerie resemblance to hers. Like the mare, I had uncomplainingly borne many burdens for an extended period of time. Similarly, my life seemed to be a constant struggle, all work and no play. This had not seemed problematic to me; I was dedicated to perseverance, to surviving whatever might come.

Certainly, I had earned my stripes as "The Responsible One." I had survived a dysfunctional, isolated childhood, handling responsibilities beyond my years. I had married young and divorced while still in my twenties, struggling to pay the bills while raising three children. Later, my second husband, Phil, was diagnosed with an incurable form of cancer, only months after we had welcomed our late in life "bonus baby," and just weeks after we moved into a new home. Soon after, I was downsized from my job and, to meet my responsibilities as both breadwinner and caretaker of my family, I decided to open my own business, working from home as a free-lance business writer.

None of this seemed unusual to me; it was simply my life. I was proud of being calm in a crisis, cool under pressure. I was the "go to" person for others in my life, and proud of it. My claim to fame was my ability to survive the slings and arrows of life, with my head unbowed. Like the old gray mare, I just kept plodding along, never considering the possibility that there was any other way to live. I smugly bragged that I would never allow myself to be victimized by negative circumstances in my life, like so many others seemed to be. My heart was scarred by the many painful events I had experienced but, like a tired old horse, I plodded along, eyes fixed straight ahead, never giving thought to any other path.

Lately, though, as I contemplated that old gray mare, I had begun to feel annoyed by her endless patience. I wanted to tell her to get a life. My patience with my own life, you see, was wearing thin. I had become sullen and resentful. I felt driven by a newfound rebelliousness. While before I had accepted additions to my load with little more than a sigh, now I itched to shake off the harness, kick over the traces and run away, into the wind.

What was the old gray mare trying to tell me? At first, I didn't know. I could see some parallels in my life, but no solutions. Yet the horse kept plodding through my mind, pulling that heavy load.

Eventually, to my horror, I recognized that being "The Responsible One" was simply another name for "victim." Because of guilt, low self-esteem and lack of goals in my life, I had taken on far more than I should have; I had accepted responsibilities that weren't truly mine. I had somehow subconsciously believed that I needed to earn my way, in my family and in the larger world, by being "good" and by taking care of others, often at the expense of taking care of myself. The result, I'm afraid, was that I became a control freak, nose appropriately cocked skyward, looking down on others for their lack of responsibility and efficiency. I also became a martyr ("OK, *fine*, I'll take care of it"). Worst of all, I was a person of unfulfilled promise, with "duty" as the excuse for never exploring and enjoying my own talents.

When I figured out the gray mare's message, I began to see more options available to me. I could spend gobs of time cooling my heels at Adversity Plaza, deeply entrenched in my comfortable "Why me?" mentality, or I could kick up my little horse hoofs, and dance my way through life. I could keep churning out PR copy until my fingers fell off, hoping someone would spring me, like Cinderella, from my drudgery, or I could gather my courage and follow my heart. Would I become a speaker, an author and whatever else I was called to be—or would I continue to hide in the "cocoon" of excuses and responsibilities with which I had filled my life? In short, I could immerse myself in the peace and abundance I knew God had designed for me, or I could continue to be the harried, worried witch I had become.

Do you want to know what happened to that old gray mare? You'll find out, near the end of the book, when you read "The Young Black Filly." (No fair peeking ahead of time.)

A Winter Story

I try not to gripe about the weather. After all, there's nothing we can do about it, so why complain? And I realize that I have it easy compared to people like my poor son, Mike, who works in construction and has spent many horrendously cold days perched precariously on the icy roof of a new house. But I have to confess: this winter seems very difficult to me. Nothing goes well. I keep dropping things because my hands are so cold. I twisted my back when I slipped on the ice. My lip balm is in constant use; static cling follows me wherever I go. I just want to curl up in an afghan on the couch and stay there.

Has it been that way for you, too, binkie? If so, let's have a little group grouch session. Repeat after me: We're tired of gray skies and bitter winds. We're tired of listening to weather reports that all say the same thing: "It's very cold, and more snow is on the way." For Pete's sake, there has been snow on the ground every single day since Christmas, and the temperatures have been stuck in the teens, seemingly for months on end . . . and this is not, after all, Alaska, or Michigan's Upper Peninsula, or Siberia!

Okay, did that little tirade help? Did it warm up your frozen blood a little? Good! Now, settle back and I'll tell you a wintertime story. It's the tale of a killer driveway, and how it was tamed.

Recently, I needed to go to the grocery store to buy brownies and other necessities. This simple task became an epic battle, woman against the elements, winner take all. I could focus on nothing else; the effort was all consuming. I knew that if I took my mind off the struggle for even a moment, I would be doomed.

Why is life so hard? This was the question on my mind as I shoveled and then salted two narrow tracks through the heavy snow in my driveway, just enough to accommodate my car's tires. My modest goal was simply to be able to drive back up the driveway when I returned from the store. If I miscalculated in my shoveling and salting, I would be left at the bottom of a steep hill, unable to even claw my way to the top, much less lug a bag of groceries up to the house. (As my husband often says, in tremendous understatement: "It's easy getting *down* our driveway; it's getting back *up* that is the problem.")

If you've ever visited my house, you know that I'm not exaggerating when I say my driveway is the worst in town. Even in summertime, people who visit are reluctant to park on our very steep driveway. Few people attend our garage sales, either. They take one look at the "mountain," realize they would be out of breath and wheezing by the time they inched their way up to the garage, smile politely, and get back in their cars. Invariably, in nice weather, everyone who comes here says, "Wow! How do you ever deal with this driveway in winter?" If people *do* come here in winter, even if it's not snowing, they often call ahead to ask, nervously, "Uh, how's your driveway today?" It is, and I mean this sincerely, the Driveway From H—E—Double Toothpicks.

My driveway's larger-than-life reputation was born during the first winter we lived in this house, ten years ago, when it tried, most outrageously, to kill my husband. On a cold January afternoon, a few weeks after we moved in, Phil fell in the driveway while shoveling snow. It wasn't a serious fall; he just slipped. But he was in terrible pain and couldn't get up. We soon learned that the reason for the intense pain was that the fall had broken a vertebra, weakened by multiple myeloma, a very inconsiderate type of cancer.

For a long time after the diagnosis, none of us could bear to think about that awful afternoon. We could hardly face shoveling snow, or even looking at the driveway. We somehow saw it as a living, monstrous entity; we actually blamed the driveway for Phil's having cancer. Not very logical, I know, but then, neither is cancer. After several awful years, Phil got better and the winters got milder and the driveway was just a driveway again, at least most of the time.

What I learned from that wintry experience is that the driveway wasn't going to change, but I could. Although I can't choose what happens, I can at least choose to find some good in it. I also learned that things can *always* be worse. So, no matter how cold it gets, no matter how many times we have to shovel and salt that driveway, I figure I can at least be glad for a few things. I have a shovel, a house and a driveway . . . and a car (once I can extricate it from the snowdrifts) that can take me on an emergency brownie run. So, let it snow. Winter's icy fingers cannot penetrate my heart, because I'm focusing on the beautiful blue sky and bright sunshine that are always just around the corner.

Goodbyes

Do you ever stop to think of how many times we say "goodbye" in a typical day? We say goodbye to our spouse as we leave for work. We say goodbye to the kids as they rush out the door, late, for the bus. We say goodbye to our co-workers as we head for home. We say goodbye to the clerk in the checkout line. We say goodbye so often, and so easily, that we may not even be aware that we're doing it.

But there are other, larger, more deeply felt farewells . . . the ones we don't want to say; the ones we don't want to feel; the ones that fill our hearts and souls with emotion. The explosive, emphatic, this-is-the-end-of-our-relationship (goodBYE!) shouted into the phone or into someone's face, when we feel hurt, when we feel cornered or badgered, or when we are simply too angry to know what else to say.

There is the tender farewell between lovers who must part, the heartfelt, "I-can-hardly-bear-it" sort of goodbye, the "it's-going-to-be-too-long-till-we're-together-again" goodbye. Similar to the lovers' goodbye is the lingering, laughing, hugging goodbye we say to dear friends and family, when the time we've spent together has been so enjoyable but, as always, too short.

This brings us to the truly unspeakable, indescribably wrenching good-byes that, eventually, all of us must face, when someone we love leaves, either voluntarily or through death. We stand there as they go, feeling alone and broken-hearted.

"Goodbye" reminds me of my late brother-in-law, Gene, who hated the word and never said it. Instead, he always said, "See ya." Even when he was dying of cancer, he didn't say goodbye to us. He just slipped quietly away.

There isn't much we can do to prepare for such painful partings—especially those that come suddenly. After the farewell comes a dark time of grief, a feeling that life will never be the same, as indeed it won't.

At such times, we can look to the wisdom of nature: the way the ocean tides ebb and flow, the flight south of birds in the winter and their return in the spring. Author Anne Morrow Lindbergh, no stranger to sorrow, wrote that "each cycle of the tide is valid; each cycle of the wave is valid; each cycle of a relationship is valid." We recall the beautiful words in Ecclesiastes: "to everything there is a season." We strive to believe this, that all experiences are valid; that each, whether painful or joyful, is simply part of life.

We see the truth of this in photographs. Each picture captures an instant in time; had we snapped the shot even a second later, the image would have been different. It is the nature of life itself to change; animals are born, then die; the seasons come and go; children grow up; we move to new homes; we change jobs; the flow of life continues. Having seen so much change in the world and in my own life, I've come to know that night won't last forever, because tomorrow's light is already present, even if I can't see it yet. Daybreak, like darkness, will come.

Of course, not all farewells are painful. Saying goodbye to an unhealthy relationship opens space for someone new to step in.

Leaving a job leads us to new adventures elsewhere. And think how much better the world would be if we chose to say goodbye to prejudice, fear, anger and retaliation, and instead said hello to peace, tranquility, faith and acceptance.

Since September 11, 2001, people have seemed turned inward, more in touch with their fears than their blessings. We seem caught up in worries about the actions of others, which of course we can never control. We seem to be dwelling on "what if's," rather than opportunities. We look over our shoulders, expecting the worst. How would things change if we expected the best, instead?

A very wise woman, who faced more grief and pain in her long life than most of us can imagine, noted that birds sing after a storm . . . so why shouldn't we? That woman was Rose Fitzgerald Kennedy, and her losses are well documented. Surely, if she could rise above her misfortunes, we can too, both personally and as a nation.

One of the most miraculous examples of hope I've ever seen was born out of the tragedy of 9/11. It is a wonderful reminder that beauty can spring forth from ruin. It is an image that shines forth radiantly, triumphantly, like new green grass after a wildfire. It is the image of the dozens and dozens of babies—babies of every race and circumstance—who were born after their fathers perished on 9/11.

Do our hearts break for them, and for their mothers? Absolutely. But the innocence of their tiny faces, the joy and hope for the future that these precious little blanketed bundles represent, lessen the pain, and life somehow seems beautiful and worthwhile once more. So, through our tears, we can be thankful again; we can feel peace in our hearts, knowing that, even after "goodbye," joy is still possible.

A Dog Tale

These days, it seems that we all need shelter from the storm. We need something to cheer about. Something heartwarming to ponder when we begin to think that civilization is going down the tubes.

I have such a story for you, about an adorable puppy named Dakota. He belonged to my sister, Terry, who got him when he was only four weeks old. We don't know how he came to be in a pet shop at that very tender age; we just know that he was lucky, indeed, to have a new "mommy" to take him in, and that he filled Terry's heart with joy.

Dakota's new home was my sister's tiny apartment. At first, the puppy was so small that the lack of space was unimportant. (Terry actually tucked him into her handbag a few times, in those early days, and took him shopping with her. He was that small.) As Dakota grew, though, it was clear that he was going to be quite a bit bigger than Terry had estimated. He was quickly outgrowing the little apartment. Simultaneously, the apartment's management set new rules for pets, stipulating a stiff monthly fee if tenants wanted to keep them.

My sister sadly realized she couldn't afford to keep Dakota, and that her tiny home wouldn't meet his needs anymore. So she began asking everyone she knew if they would adopt him. She asked them to spread the word to others, too. She prayed for a good outcome, even as she grieved having to give up her dog.

I was amazed at how many people took the time to help. Several people visited Dakota, but either they or Terry determined the fit wasn't quite right. Many kind souls suggested solutions, but nothing worked out. Emails poured in from people who couldn't take him, but wanted us to know they cared. As the deadline approached, my sister faced the grim possibility that she might have to relinquish Dakota to a shelter or dog pound.

But finally, a solution: through my business, I met a kind-hearted dog lover named Michelle. She had great empathy for my sister, knowing how hard it must be to give up her dog. Michelle herself already had two dogs, two cats, three children, a husband and a busy job. She mentioned that she had a large yard with plenty of room for an active puppy, and said she would be glad to be Dakota's foster mom until a home could be found. She was certain she could place him. She said it would be her pleasure.

All that remained was to see if Dakota would feel comfortable with Michelle and her family, and vice versa. Terry bathed and shampooed Dakota within an inch of his life. We packed up his favorite toys and drove to Michelle's house, nervously, but with hope in our hearts. Along the way, Terry lectured Dakota, as any mom would, about being a good boy. Despite Dakota's charming personality, Terry was worried because he had never been around other dogs, and hadn't had many human visitors either. Would he be terrified? Would he bite someone? Would he piddle on Michelle's nice carpet?

If Michelle ever chooses to name her home, she should call it "Sanctuary," because that is what it is. Terry and I, and young Dakota, were enveloped with caring and kindness the minute we stepped inside. The puppy bonded immediately with Michelle and her kids, especially 12-year-old Stephen. Both on the cusp of their teens, they were kindred souls. Next, one by one, the family's two dogs were brought in to check out the newcomer. Both Bailey, the protective older dog, and Angus, a feisty youngster about Dakota's age, were graciously accepting, each in their own way. Even the cats checked out the guest, from a safe distance.

Dakota at first seemed frozen in bewilderment; a touch of fear was evident in his brown eyes. Soon, though, he ventured bravely towards the other dogs, to sniff noses. A moment later, he was frolicking joyously with the welcoming committee. We were witnessing the exact moment when he realized he was a dog, that there were others like him in the world, and that they would be his friends. It was truly a spiritual moment.

As Terry and I said good-bye, a bit sadly but knowing that Dakota would be well cared for, we felt overwhelmed by the generosity we had just experienced. Even if a magic wand were at our disposal, we couldn't have created a better, more loving situation for Dakota. (Update: Dakota continues to live, zestfully and permanently, with Michelle and her family, in what I can only think of as Dog Heaven.)

The world must be in better shape than we sometimes think it is, if one little dog's plight can matter so much, to the scores of people who tried to help, and to his eventual new family. It is said that one can judge a culture by how it treats its old, its sick, its young, its furry ones—those who can't fend for themselves. If Dakota's story is an example, it would seem that, in the long run, peace and love will continue to prevail over ignorance and hate, somehow.

Remember Dakota's story, whenever you need hope. Believe that, as long as there are Michelles, the Dakotas (and our world) will thrive. And all of us will be just a little better off for knowing that this is so. Reach out, when you can, to the least among us. Doing so, you will encounter the best that any of us can ever hope to be.

Irish Blessing

"May the road rise up to meet you.
May the wind be always at your back.
May the sun shine warm upon your face,
The rains fall soft upon your fields,
And, until we meet again,
May God hold you in the palm of His hand."

Such a beautiful blessing, isn't it? I have always loved it, and believed that its simple sentiments provide a gentle benediction to everyone who reads it. It had personal meaning to me, too, because it had been read during our wedding ceremony in 1984. That's why, when we moved into our new home, in late 1992, I bought a nicely framed version of it to hang in our foyer to greet all who entered our home.

But there was a delay of many months—more than a year—before the day came when I hung my Irish Blessing on the foyer wall. We had only unpacked the most essential items when we moved into the house, and didn't bother hanging pictures, since it was December and the busy Christmas season was upon us. I thought I would have ample time to finish emptying boxes and decorating the house in January. But it was not to be. Just after Christmas, Phil was diagnosed with multiple myeloma, an incurable form of cancer . . . and nothing has ever been the same.

At various times during the nightmarish days and nights of that first year or so, it occurred to me that I should try to find the time and energy to hang a few pictures and unpack a few more boxes . . . make the house more homey. But everything felt so temporary, so tentative, to me, that it was hard to even contemplate working on the house. I felt as if I didn't have a home, because so much that was home to me had been destroyed, and because the house itself had been the scene of so much pain, so many tears. One day, my tired mind even decided the house was somehow cursed; that it would never really belong to us. And the energy it would take to fix up the house, I believed, was energy that was needed for taking care of my children, earning money to keep the house and, of course, helping Phil keep the cancer at bay.

One day, however, I noticed the framed Irish Blessing, now quite dusty, perched on top of a box of mementos. I carefully cleaned it, found a hammer and pounded in a nail, feeling a bit more cheerful as I worked. Then I hung the picture and stepped back to admire it. I reached out to straighten it a bit, only to have it crash to the floor. The glass under the frame shattered, scattering bits of broken glass all over the tile floor.

I stood there in utter shock . . . and tremendous anger. I tried to tell myself, "It's okay; it can be fixed." But some things cannot be repaired. Suddenly, I dissolved into a paroxysm of tears, crying as if I would never stop. As I looked at the shattered bits of glass on the floor, I saw them as my heart, broken into bits over my inability to save Phil—and myself—from this dreadful illness. I saw my four children's faces among the glass fragments—why couldn't I have somehow spared them the pain they were now experiencing? Wasn't that my job, as their mother?

I saw my cherished dreams—that Phil and I would raise our baby, Andrew, together; that we would joyously attend the older kids' weddings; that we would grow old together in this house that we had called our dream house—all lying on the floor in those broken pieces of glass. The sharp-edged fragments littering the floor somehow ignited the feelings of rage and fear I carried inside, the anger I felt at having my life turned upside down by the disease, entirely against my will, the fear of the future that haunted my days and nights. The tinkling sound of the glass hitting the floor somehow became tiny voices that mocked me, saying, "Even this, the Irish Blessing, you shall be denied. Even this, you shall not have."

Everyone had marveled at my ability to carry the load, to raise a baby while walking with Phil through this crisis, to run a business, guide Kerry through her last days of high school, to take care of everything and everybody. I had been grateful for that ability, too. I had prided myself on keeping my act together. I had cried, of course, but never like this. Now, all the pent-up emotion burst forth like a river rushing over a dam. I cried in torrents. I ranted and raved. In despair, I cried out to God: "Why, since I can't have the thing I most want—which I don't even dare ask you for, which I've accepted I cannot have—*why* can't I at least have one moment of normalcy, why can't I have this blessing on my wall?"

For a long time after that day, there was silence within me, the calm after the storm. But eventually, slowly and painstakingly, the road did rise up to meet me once again, the ruts temporarily smoothed, the way clear. The wind was at my back, supporting me, instead of in front of me, pushing me back. On some days, the sun was warm on my tear-stained face, and the rains fell more softly on my tired, desolate fields, and I began to realize that, no matter what, God still holds me, lovingly, so very lovingly, in the palm of his hand. And the Irish Blessing hangs on my foyer wall.

What's Your Season?

Here in northeastern Ohio, we get to experience the wonders of all four seasons—sometimes, seemingly, in a single day! We admire the pristine beauty of winter's snow and ice. We never take sunshine for granted; in spring, we drop what we're doing to marvel at the first, tiny bits of green poking up through the brown earth. We savor the warm days and delicious sense of freedom that summer brings. We drink in the splendor of fall, when the leaves put on their incredible color show.

Sometimes, however, it can seem that we're at the mercy of the seasons. Picnics can be spoiled if it rains; ice on the roads causes accidents and school closings; spring rains can cause flooding; summertime can be oppressively hot. But we can enjoy whatever season we are in, regardless of the weather, if we choose to.

This also applies to seasons of the heart. When we find ourselves in such seasons, we often feel (just as with Mother Nature) that we're at their mercy. We have experiences we don't choose. We are unexpectedly thrown into winter's cold; we can feel blindsided by summer's fierce, sudden heat. Certainly the early days of my husband's struggle with cancer seemed dark, cold and wintry to us. When he began to get better, we had many intense, exhilarating spring moments. In the last few years, we've experienced the sunny glow of summertime more and more often. And of course, we know that autumn, full of both beauty and loss, is always just around the corner.

But in reality, what changed over time, mostly, was our attitude. Today, as in the wintry early days, Phil still has an incurable disease, and it is not in remission. But somehow, we began to choose the season we wanted—kind of like deciding to go to Florida in wintertime. On occasions when we couldn't quite get ourselves into the season (attitude) we wanted, we decided to at least find something good in the season we were given.

For instance, on the darkest days, when winter had an icy grip on our hearts, when things seemed hopeless, we were still able, sometimes, to see the beauty of this cold season. We saw it in the love of our family and friends, the care of the nurses and doctors at the hospital and, often, in the kindness of strangers. On some dark, cold days we succeeded in enjoying winter, feeling a rush of excitement, just at being together, that was rather like the exhilaration of a walk on a crystal-cold January day.

Springtime, of course, is a bit tricky. We can go along thinking sunshine and blue skies are here for good, when instead they may disappear at a moment's notice, leaving us vulnerable to yet another cruel blast of winter. Our cancer odyssey has been like that. We have been filled with euphoria, that heady rush of new energy that is spring, only to have our hopes dashed, as Old Man Winter roared back in. That's when we would be thankful for any spring-like moments we could find—the ridiculous singing Valentine socks I gave Phil when he was in the hospital, the moments when he could shuffle down the hall, dragging his IV tree with him. We can choose our season, and we chose spring.

Ah, summer! That long, mellow time when things seem slower-paced, the living is easy and the landscape is a feast for our eyes. That's the season we yearn for, isn't it? The beautiful blossoms, the barbecues and picnics. How could anything ugly intrude on a summer's day? But, just like a mosquito sneaking through a window screen, it can, and when it does, "the seasonal choice" is yours again. Will you remain in summer, or will you yield to dark, winter attitudes? Will you stay at Adversity Plaza, or will you hail the taxi? Sometimes remaining in summer takes courage, because you are in danger of deluding yourself that fall will never come. But with an attitude of gratitude, with the desire to see only flowers and sunshine, summer can be with you always.

But doesn't each moment of summer bring us ever closer to the bare-tree, gray sky days of late fall and early winter? Yes, but that is the price we gladly pay for those glorious days. And we don't need to focus on the losses ahead; instead, I prefer to notice the splendor of autumn, the stunning colors that the dying leaves offer us. How amazing that, each year, the trees save their very best for last! How healthy they are, celebrating their moment of finality by painting the town red (and yellow, orange, burgundy and brown), rather than grieving what is to come! That, to me, is comforting, and breathtakingly honest. And, besides, in due time, after the bare-tree days and the long winter nights, springtime will return. It always does.

What are the seasons of your heart? Do you welcome each one? Can you find the good in each of them? Which season do you choose?

Up and At 'Em When You're Down and Out

Have you ever had a series of experiences so frustrating, so seemingly negative, that you just wanted to host a gigantic pity party for yourself? Have you ever wanted to throw in the towel, because everything seemed endlessly bleak? Have you ever, to use a phrase my mother often invoked at such times, wanted to jump into a hole and pull the hole in after you?

That is exactly where I am right now. I am in a major funk. I'm talking a double-dyed blue mood so dark it's almost black. I'm talking such a frustrated and foul attitude that I long for a desert island . . . as do, no doubt, those who have to put up with me. Or maybe Fantasy Island would be even better—someplace where I can create a world that's just perfect (at least for me). I yearn for a quiet place to lick my wounds, throw a fit and eat potato chips (which is my style of going on a bender).

We're talking a hissy fit of impressive magnitude. I just want to get off this merry-go-round, take a hike, and get away from everybody and everything. A Calgon-style "take me away" bubble bath will not suffice. Not even the appearance of a dashing, take-charge Rhett Butler type (should one show up) would do the trick. Even chocolate, my most dependable lifesaver of all, is of no use. This is an "I have had it, dyed in the wool, ain't gonna take it no more, that's not a light at the end of the tunnel, it's an oncoming train" level of the blues. I am, most profoundly, in the pits.

What's that you say? This is supposed to be an upbeat, encouraging, even inspirational story? Sigh. Okay, I will try to drag myself up out of the pit long enough to see if there's any daylight breaking through that I can share with you. First, though, I must say that others can be *so annoying* when we're acres deep in feeling sorry for ourselves. For example, we are often advised to pull ourselves up by the bootstraps—even when we are, metaphorically speaking, barefoot. And some well-meaning friend is sure to remind us of our blessings and suggest we count them—not realizing our blessing calculator is temporarily out of batteries. Another sigh . . .

So, what to do? My first, snippy response to my own question is to say, "How would I know?" Then, a little voice inside whispers, "You *do* know. You just don't want to do it. And your job is to brighten up the day for your readers, so get cracking!" All right, all right. But I can't do this on my own in my present mood. So we'll let the "little voice" inside do most of the talking.

And what a pest that little twerp can be! Just as I've got a real tirade going in my head, about how unfair life is, how difficult, how frustrating it can be, the voice pipes up to say, "Name 10 people who have it worse than you do—right now." So I go through that mental exercise, which I must confess didn't take long at all. I must concede that many—literally *millions*—of people have a more difficult life than I do.

Next, the annoyance within says, "Let's find some silver linings in your problems. What good can come out of the negative situations you're experiencing?" What a dumb question. If there was good in there, would I be in a funk? "Ahem!" the voice says. And so I stubbornly concede that good times always follow bad ones. And I reluctantly recall the words of the great Middle Eastern philosopher, Kahlil Gibran, who tells us that when sorrow breaks our hearts, the hollowed-out heart is then more open to love; has a greater capacity for love. Judging from the many big-hearted people I know, virtually all of whom have experienced great sorrow at some point in their lives, this seems to be true.

Never content to rest on her laurels, the infernal internal whisperer says, "And don't you acquire greater strength, deeper insights, from the bad as well as from the good?" Hmmm. I suppose so, though I don't see why we can't learn 'em in some easier way. All I know is, if recent episodes in my life are character building, I'll soon be a *real* character!

In her silkiest tones, the mosquito within says, "And if you didn't have funks, how would you experience the love and support that your friends and family shower on you whenever you need it? How would you realize how precious you are to others?" As I try desperately to swat her voice out of my brain, I reluctantly admit that she is right, yet again. Care and concern pour in from so many kind folks, usually without my even asking for it. I am truly blessed, which I suppose is what the irritating little voice is always trying to help me recognize.

And so, as I wistfully watch the leaves falling, instead of dreading winter I can recognize that each day brings me closer to spring. As I grieve for the pain and uncertainty facing my beloved brother, who was diagnosed with cancer on September 11, 2001, I can recall that many others faced worse grief that day. As I agonize over career options, I can recognize that I've been blessed with certain talents and abilities, and trust that I'll find ways to use them. As I fuss about a shortage of cash, I can humbly recognize how wealthy I am, compared to most of the world's people. And as I contemplate Thanksgiving, I realize I had better start counting my blessings right now, because my list is so long the turkey will be cold long before I finish expressing my gratitude. Here's hoping your list is equally impressive.

This One's for You, Mom

She was a multi-faceted woman: intelligent, private, with an avid interest in music and the arts, devoutly religious, a diehard political liberal . . . and a diehard Ohio State Buckeyes football and basketball fan. She had an incorrigible sweet tooth, and an equally incorrigible interest in soap operas. She was generous with what few worldly goods she possessed. She was sensitive to the needs of others, especially the poor and the sick, and had a wondrous capacity for forgiveness. She possessed great courage in facing difficulties, probably because she had so much practice. Most of all, she was kind, loving and gentle. She was my mother, Catherine Amicon Burdick, who died in 1986.

Of course, Mom had many other qualities, some more endearing than others. She had an irritating way of clearing her throat that drove me up the wall. She was fascinated with the weather even though, since she seldom left the house, one would think she had little need to be concerned about it. Ah, but no. She listened to every weather report, particularly in winter, and would call to report the gory details to me. I don't know if she thought I didn't notice the weather, or if she believed that only she was qualified to offer me a detailed analysis of meteorological data. When heavy snow was predicted, for example, she would hint to me that perhaps I should stay home—as if I could call off work each time it snowed!

I bought her groceries for her, and her shopping lists made me crazy. She was extremely precise about what she wanted. Each item had to be a specific brand—no substitutions, please. She also loved trying new products that she saw on television—except that sometimes they weren't yet available locally. Even if I had looked for the item at several different stores (usually with three small, cranky children in tow), I always had the uneasy feeling that she thought I hadn't looked hard enough. I will not even try to describe the frustration that ensued (on both sides) when one of Mom's favorite cosmetics was suddenly no longer available. Or my incredulity as to how one woman could go through so much toilet paper in only a week.

Mom was the youngest of ten children born to Italian immigrants in Columbus, Ohio. The family, even today, is vociferous, warm, witty and opinionated. (If you are of Italian heritage yourself, you know that last sentence is a vast understatement of fact.) Mom, though, was a bit less intense than the rest. I'm not sure why. Perhaps, by the time they welcomed their 10th child, my grandparents' feisty Italian genes had begun to mellow. Whatever it was, Mom seemed to march to a different drummer.

She certainly didn't lack the family determination (read: stubbornness), but she went at things a bit differently. For instance, she didn't get married young, as most of her siblings did. Instead, she became a nurse and worked at a large, inner city hospital. She spent years in the emergency room, patching up crooks, prostitutes, accident victims and police officers, yet somehow maintaining an innocence and a faith in humankind that seemed naïve, considering her experiences.

She wanted desperately to enlist as an Army or Navy nurse during World War II, but she was repeatedly turned down, both because of health problems and because she was "vertically challenged." Wearing her highest heels and her most commanding attitude, she tried valiantly to convince the recruitment officer that she was, indeed, 5'2" tall, but to no avail. Mom also explored becoming a nun. Eventually, she determined she had not been called to serve in that way and returned to nursing, much to the benefit of the many patients she served over the years.

So, long before it was popular, even though she came from a very traditional background, Mom was a career woman—actually a renaissance woman of varied interests and talents. She loved to dance and sing and was a masterful pianist. She was also a talented writer, producing plays in which her hospital colleagues starred.

The second half of my mother's life, however, was quite a dichotomy from the first. At the late age (in her era) of 35, she became a mother—to me and, in due time, to my sister and brother. She endured a difficult marriage, a chronic heart condition that often kept her bedridden, and few diversions—seemingly a sad departure from her earlier life. However, even as I write this, I can hear her saying, "Oh, Kathy, many others had a harder life than mine. I had my precious children, and I had God."

She was a wonderful mother. Our family life would undoubtedly be termed "dysfunctional" today, but we were rich in love. Mom would wrap up little treasures as surprises for us, showing us the importance of celebrations and generosity. She brightened our modest home with inexpensive knickknacks, throw rugs (strategically placed to cover splintery floorboards) and plants. Her creativity found expression in making us great Halloween costumes, and in cooking and baking. Her culinary talents, I'm sure, were the inspiration for the term "comfort food."

Mom encouraged us to read, and managed to obtain many books for us. She taught us to be honest, respectful, and kind, and to believe that prayer conquers all. As we watched the civil rights movement unfolding on television, she taught us that all people deserve freedom, that even as children we could forward this cause by our own behavior, and that even those who would deny others freedom deserved forgiveness, whether we understood why or not. She taught us that music, autumn leaves and unexpected moments of joy in everyday life are God moments, and that love is the answer, no matter what the question.

And so, Mom, I cherish my memories of you, with love and gratitude. I thank you for making everything out of nothing, day after day, for protecting and guiding us as best you could, and for giving us daily examples of patience, honor, generosity and courage. Thanks, too, for your shortcomings, idiosyncrasies and quirks, which annoyed the heck out of me, and which I have inherited in spades. Take care, sweet mother. I'll be seeing you, in autumn leaves, in majestic music, in my children's faces, and in every unexpected little joy that comes along.

Second Stop:

The Gallery of Shattered Dreams

The Gallery is our next stop. As you peek inside, at first you may see only despair, pain and frustration. You notice only dusty paintings hanging on dirty walls; you see only the broken dreams, the sagging spirits, the tarnished glory that the abandoned artwork represents. You may be tempted to turn away, thinking that only sadness lives here.

Eventually, though, as you strain your eyes to see what's inside, you will recognize that, even in shattered dreams, hope resides. Paintings can be cleaned, floors can be swept; yesterday's beauty—or tomorrow's creativity—can spring forth. You will find that, even when you don't get what you want in life, you get something of great value, if you are open to seeing it.

*　　*　　*

Change

Change. Such a simple word. Most people, at least initially, seem to view change as a negative. Think about it: if your boss says, "I've changed my mind" about a project you're working on, don't you immediately think, "Uh oh. All that work I did was just a waste of time"? If she says, "We're changing gears around here," your first thought might be, "I could lose my job." Certainly in the workplace there is trepidation and even fear about change, regardless of how positive that change might end up being. Even a move from a tiny cubicle into a plush office can give rise to concerns.

Actually, the word "workplace" is becoming almost synonymous with "change." Technological changes. Policy changes. Transfers to other cities. Changes in management. Changes in staff. Changes in corporate direction. Changes when the company announces layoffs or closings. Changes you need to make in your work ethic or attitude. Change, indeed, is the name of the game.

How about changes at home? How we choose to view them is a choice. You decide whether it is a negative—or an opportunity—when your spouse says, "It's your turn to change the baby!" Or perhaps your spouse asks if you would cook dinner for a change. Do you leap to your feet and run joyously to the kitchen? Probably not.

I consider myself something of a change expert, so I understand why we usually see change in a negative light. Ten years ago, practically everything in my life changed with dizzying speed. Within one year's time, my husband and I had a "late in life" baby, we left a support group that had been our main source of friends and social activities, and we moved (much to the chagrin of my teenaged daughter) into a new home.

Soon after, I left a highly visible full-time job for a low-profile part-time one, my husband, Phil, was diagnosed with an incurable form of cancer, the company I worked for was sold—which meant that just as I became our sole breadwinner, I lost my job. The following year was no better. My husband had to retire from his job because of his illness, I started a home-based writing business to support us, while simultaneously trying to determine how I would fund my daughter's upcoming college education. And, worst of all, Phil's brother was also diagnosed with cancer (and later passed away).

Now, you might ask, where am I going with this? Certainly not to a pity party, or even to the funny farm, believe it or not. The personal examples are simply meant to underscore these points: Change is going to occur *constantly*, whether you like it or not. Good changes can initially seem negative. Even bad changes will bring *some* good.

Did I accept all this change in my life willingly? Heck, no! I was furious. I ranted and raved in my "discussions" with God. I went on a years-long potato chip binge, often complemented by a glass of whine (and even some wine). I roared like a tiger caught in a net, railing against my fate. I did not submit graciously. But, in time, I learned many valuable lessons from the unwelcome changes in my life.

Life is meant to wax and wane. A flower grows, buds, blooms, and dies. A baby is born, grows up, grows old, and passes away.

Nothing ever does—indeed, *cannot*—stay the same. Change is one of the few absolutes in life.

How can we cope with never knowing what is next? We can *embrace* change. For example, if you hoped for sunshine but got showers instead, slip off your shoes and go wading in the mud puddles. If you have gained weight you can't lose in time for a big event, just buy a new tie or a new dress and be comfortable in the skin you're in. A bit more challenging: when someone you love leaves you behind, savor the good times you enjoyed together, forgive him/her and look ahead to the "someone new" who is just around the corner.

Not so easy to embrace change? No, but it's always rewarding. If we can gradually develop a mindset that welcomes change (or at least accepts it), if we focus as much as possible on taking satisfaction in meeting the challenges, we'll find a silver lining in there somewhere.

If you simply can't find that silver lining, at least reserve the concept in your mind that some good *might* be hidden inside. Does this attitude, this embracing of change, mean that you will never again be frustrated by change? Absolutely not! But try to remember that, just as the ocean's tides ebb and flow, this negative change will lose its sting, to be replaced by something more positive that will soon flow into your life.

We are meant to learn and grow in response to change . . . and then learn some more. A wise philosopher once said that if you aren't busy growing, you're busy dying. All around us is evidence that this is true. So *live. Grow.* Invite change into your hearts.

Driving Blind

I often wonder how I ever got home alive. Day after day, night after night, after my husband was diagnosed with cancer, I drove to the hospital and then home again. Endlessly making my rounds, from the familiar streets of my small town, onto the expressway, to the city streets, to the hospital parking deck. Later, daily, I made the same trek back home again. And as I drove, I cried.

On the way to the hospital, I would cry about leaving my baby at home, when I wanted so much to hold him. And I would cry over my teenaged daughter, whose carefree youth had been so suddenly and brutally cut short, and my two older sons, tall and strong on the outside, but hurting, I knew, on the inside.

As I left the hospital each evening, after spending as much time with Phil as I could, the tears began again. This time I cried over Phil's helplessness and pain, his loss of independence and dignity, my fear of losing him, and my grief over what we had already lost. And I cried for myself.

I marveled that one could weep so much, and so often. It seemed the tears came automatically, as soon as I turned the key in the ignition of the car. Eventually, I came to realize that this time in the car was the only time I could grieve freely and completely, without taking time from those who needed me, without frightening the kids with the depth of my feelings. And so I cried as I drove.

So often, before cancer, I used to mutter under my breath about others' driving. I was so impatient with their speed—or lack of it. Now I bless them as I pass by, knowing that they may have just left a sickbed or a deathbed, knowing they may be driving blind, through tears that I cannot see. Agonies are often hidden away, politely cloaked, as we go through our daily lives. But now I know that every day someone whom I encounter is, unknown to me, struggling with inner demons. And I try to be kind.

Lilacs: To Have and To Hold

Lilacs have very special meaning to me. They remind me of my mother, who died years ago. Many trees and flowers surrounded the house where I grew up. The lilacs are what I remember most vividly: that sweet, rich fragrance, the plump purple and white clusters. Just the smell of lilacs carries me home again. I remember taking huge clusters of lilacs to school each May. I remember my mother making generous bouquets for us to deliver to our neighbors; and I remember sitting among the lilac bushes, drinking in their delicious scent as I played in the grass. To me, lilacs have always symbolized the innocence of childhood and the bountiful beauty of springtime. But now, because of my husband's gift, lilacs mean even more.

When we first moved into our house, less than three months before my birthday, as Phil and I walked around our back yard, I mentioned that I would like to get some lilac bushes to plant in the spring. Though I didn't know it then, this was one of the last "normal" conversations we would have for quite some time because Phil was diagnosed with cancer just a few weeks later.

Our lives were forever changed. Following diagnosis, Phil was in the hospital for nearly six weeks while undergoing orthopedic surgery and other treatments. When he came home at last, he was frail, thin, wearing a back brace and using a walker. I had nearly forgotten my approaching birthday, but my children had gotten a cake and invited a few friends over. Phil was dressed in an old flannel shirt and a pair of baggy sweat pants, looking like a shadow of his former self. He was still in the throes of recovering from surgery—and accepting the diagnosis. He was also soon to face extensive chemotherapy. As you can imagine, I was not expecting anything from Phil for my birthday. So I was surprised when he slowly inched his way over to me with his walker, clutching a small, unwrapped cardboard jewelry box, which he placed on the table in front of me.

Lifting the box, and feeling its weight, I knew that it didn't contain jewelry. It was an old box, probably left over from Christmas. Opening it, I found a small, hand-scribbled note that simply said, "4 lilac bushes." I look at Phil questioningly. He said that his gift to me would be a bit delayed, until he was strong enough to go and get it. His present, he told me, was four small lilacs, to represent each of our four children. Some weeks later, our friend, John Dvorak, drove Phil to the nursery and helped him pick out the plants, which John then planted for us in the back yard.

Some women receive diamonds, cruises, or expensive works of art as gifts from their husbands; very nice, I'm sure, but not nearly as significant as Phil's gift to me. He gave me what I most needed that day: hope for the future and a promise that we would live each day together as fully as possible, for as long as possible.

Diaper Rash

You often hear people remark that one crucial moment "changed my life forever," or that "nothing has ever been the same." In the old days, BC (Before Cancer), I would mentally rebut such comments, thinking, "Yeah, right . . . *nothing's* been the same? That's got to be an exaggeration."

I am now acutely aware that some moments, some events *do* change life forever. In some instances nothing *is* ever the same again. And if there is anything that fits this category of life-altering experiences, it's having cancer come to live at your house.

Cancer is so often viewed as a crisis—especially the moment of diagnosis and the moment of death. But just as most people don't realize that many good moments can occur during the struggle, they don't realize the many ways that cancer hurts, how it eats away at every single area of life. Nothing is left untouched.

A perfect example of this is . . . diaper rash. My husband was diagnosed with cancer when our son, Andrew, was only seven months old, instantly making our child the source of our greatest grief, as well as our greatest joy. Everything we felt, saw, touched, or dreamed seemed devastating in those dark early days. Everything was suddenly fraught with new, deeper meanings.

Phil was hospitalized 14 times in the first 12 months of his illness, so I struggled to take proper care of both him and Andrew, trundling off to the hospital every day alone, often splicing together childcare arrangements by phone from Phil's room. On the days that Phil was well enough, or when my hunger for my child could no longer be ignored, I would take Andrew and his playpen to the hospital with me. Either way, each evening I drove home, exhausted and emotionally drained, only to repeat the process again the next day.

Very early in Phil's illness, when I arrived one evening at the baby sitter's to pick Andrew up, she told me she was concerned about his diaper rash. Since Cathy was a seasoned veteran, both a mom herself and an experienced childcare provider, I knew the fact that she was mentioning it was significant. We had been treating the rash with a usually effective cream for several days, but I was so harried I hadn't noticed, until Cathy mentioned it, that one area had begun to worsen.

Since Andrew is my fourth child, I'm usually unflappable about childhood ailments. But cancer *does* change everything, even diaper rash. I took Andrew home and found myself sobbing as I changed his diaper and carefully applied diaper rash ointment. As my daughter, Kerry (then 16), tried to reassure me, I begged Andrew's forgiveness for neglecting him. I prayed to God to keep my baby safe. After tucking Andrew into his crib, I got up constantly during the night to see if he was all right. Early in the morning, I called the doctor's office, explaining that Phil was in the hospital and that I needed an immediate appointment for Andrew so that I could get back to Phil's bedside.

As we waited at the doctor's office, I grew more and more panicky. I was haunted by images of Andrew's rash, which in my tortured mind had assumed life-threatening proportions. I kept thinking that Phil could die while I was sitting in this room, unable to protect him. Torn between Andrew's needs and Phil's, I learned in those anguished moments what hell is, and that we experience it here, in our hearts and mind, not in some nebulous afterlife.

And then, the last straw: a nurse came out and said that the doctor was not going to be able to see us after all. He had been called away on an emergency. My much-vaunted reputation as a calm, rational person was instantly destroyed. I simply snapped. Standing there in a room full of strangers, to my horror I began to cry. I sobbed, "Don't you understand? My baby's rash is awful and he needs to be seen and my husband has just been diagnosed with cancer and I *must* get to the hospital and I can't come here again won't somebody please help me? Please help me. Please!"

The nurse ushered us into an exam room. She was kindness incarnate. She spoke to both Andrew and me in a soothing voice. She examined Andrew carefully. She asked me about Phil's illness. She gave me a prescription for Andrew. She assured me that he would be all right, and that I had not neglected him. There are angels on earth, you see, and many of them are nurses.

Be gentle with those who are struggling with any sort of chronic or serious illness, please. Understand that, in some strange way, though one may be able to face the larger issue with courage and faith, the small ones sometimes bring you, unexpectedly, to your knees. The tiniest things, especially if they involve your precious child, who may be left fatherless, become so large that they embody all the fear and desperation that is hidden underneath. Things are not what they seem, sometimes.

Healing Ocean Breezes

I will never forget that moment. My husband, Phil, stood on the beach of the Atlantic Ocean, his shorts-clad white legs so thin, so fragile, that they looked like matchsticks, his oversized tee shirt flapping in the wind. Next to him danced Andrew, dark brown eyes aglow and honey-brown curls bouncing, laughing up at Phil and pointing excitedly at the seagulls swooping overhead. I have never in my life seen a more beautiful sight. And even now, years later, I continue to thank God for it.

It was 1996, and Andrew was four years old. I had been yearning to go to the ocean, which to me is the most wondrous place on earth to be. My last ocean visit had been in 1984, so it certainly was high time to return. And I had scrimped and saved to try to afford it. However, Phil had cancer, and when you're dealing with a serious illness, nothing is ever simple.

For one thing, reservations for seaside accommodations generally have to be made long in advance. We couldn't afford to lose the money if Phil ended up being unable to travel . . . and since we couldn't predict the next 12 days, how could we possibly predict the next 12 months? In a strange way, even the act of deciding to go seemed like tempting fate. We had learned from hard experience not to plan ahead, not to even think ahead. Often, it was too painful. Always, it was too uncertain.

Phil worried about the money and whether he would be well enough for the long car trip. I worried about what I would do if

Phil had a health crisis while we were away from home, so far from our support system. What if he got another infection? The merest sore throat can be life threatening for people with multiple myeloma. Ugly images kept flashing, unbidden, through my mind. What if something happened to Phil before the trip? Was it worth it to try to go? My tired mind kept repeating the same scenario, like an endless TV rerun: "Hello, I'm calling to cancel our vacation at your condo because my husband has died." It just didn't seem worth the risk.

But eventually, the tug of the ocean and our usual stubborn response to the illness—*Don't try to stop us from living our lives together as fully and for as long as we possibly can*—kicked in. We booked the condo and took the trip. What a triumph it was to stand there on the shore . . . together! It felt as if we'd won the lottery, an Olympic gold medal and the Kentucky Derby, all rolled in to one!

That, of course, is one of the little-known secrets about living with cancer or other serious problems. There are, thank God, compensations. Those who suffer much also enjoy much. The risks you take, simply to live a normal life, are rewarded. Cancer makes you savor everything . . . *e v e r y t h i n g!* The ocean's roar, the wind on your face, your child's delight as he builds a sand castle, the waves tickling your toes, the screech of seagulls—all are joyous, miraculous beyond description. Cancer may do its worst, but you can wrench from it life's very best.

The Pearl of Great Price

Our tenth wedding anniversary was approaching. Having never made it to double digits in my first marriage, and having experienced various stresses and strains in this marriage, I had always looked forward to celebrating this particular milestone. Since Phil's first marriage had lasted ten years, I joked that I would become a "viable" wife only after passing the ten-year mark. So, for many reasons, this anniversary had been greatly anticipated.

However, that anticipation had been snuffed out, like a candle in the wind, when Phil was diagnosed with multiple myeloma, just two months after our eighth anniversary. At that point, all of the special moments—birthdays, holidays, vacations—that had previously been joyous became, at best, bittersweet; all the irritations and frustrations of life, somehow, became precious memories. Think about it: what kind of birthday card do you buy for someone when you believe it may be his last birthday? How can you feel joy, watching your 2-year-old attempting to blow out the candles on his birthday cake, while his father is fighting back tears, wondering if he will be present for his son's *next* birthday?

So, we approached our tenth anniversary with mixed feelings. We wanted to celebrate and honor our marriage, but we knew it would also be painful. The ninth anniversary, after all, had been awful. It took place less than a year after Phil's diagnosis, at a time when the cancer was not responding to treatment and the future looked bleak. However, it didn't seem right to let the illness to have the upper hand, to allow it to prevent us from enjoying our anniversary. So we had gone out to dinner to celebrate. We began in a festive mood, but, like a balloon slowly drifting to earth as the helium escapes, we became more somber as the night wore on. It was a difficult evening.

And now, the tenth anniversary loomed. The myeloma was still not responding to treatment, not even a bone marrow transplant that Phil had recently undergone. We were one and one-half years into an incurable illness. What to do?

We decided, once again, to tough it out. We decided that we had much to celebrate, and that the cancer would not be allowed to rob us of marking this special milestone. We booked a room at a hotel and made a reservation at Giovanni's, a wonderful restaurant where we had eaten on our honeymoon. We decided to exchange gifts, but had determined that, this time, they must be very special, very symbolic.

All during dinner, I anticipated my gift from Phil. I had an idea, you see, of what it would be. We had stopped at an upscale jewelry store a couple of months previously, on our way home from one of Phil's checkups at the Cleveland Clinic. As always, I was trying to find a silver lining and decided visiting this fancy store would cheer us up. I had spied a lovely, not-too-expensive pearl ring there, and showed it to Phil. Now, I sensed that he had bought it for our anniversary.

I was right, although, in typical Phil fashion, he didn't present it to me at the swanky restaurant, with candlelight and music creating a romantic backdrop. Instead, he simply handed it to me, later on, in our hotel room. But the ring itself isn't "the pearl of great price."

As you may know, when you've been married a long time, you tend to take each other for granted. You tend to only half-listen to your partner sometimes. You tend not to notice the little things anymore—except maybe the annoying ones. But for us, cancer had changed all that. Cancer, and the threat of loss, made each moment so precious.

As we enjoyed our evening at Giovanni's, I found myself hanging on Phil's every word. I realized how priceless each sentence, each moment, really was. I tried to memorize Phil's smile, the way he pronounced certain words, the tilt of his head as he drank from his glass. I pushed away all sad thoughts, all petty irritations, and concentrated on the *now*. What beauty there was, now that I could experience it! How splendid to simply be together! What a victory it was, after such hard times, to be able to savor our anniversary, reminiscing about our years together, even though we knew this could be our last such celebration.

We had turned a corner, you see. Even though the future still looked dark, we had learned that cancer could not touch the present . . . and that the present is all we really have anyway. I suppose that must be why it's called the "present." It is a gift. It is the pearl of great price.

See Ya, Gene

One day, my husband's older brother, Gene, called and said: "Phil . . . cashews!" "Cashews?" my husband repeated. Gene went on to explain that, for the first time since he had begun chemotherapy for non-Hodgkins lymphoma, something tasted the way it used to. That "something" was cashews.

My husband and his brother had always been quite fond of each other, in a decidedly non-touchy-feely way. They particularly enjoyed having friendly arguments about politics. But it wasn't until they both were diagnosed with cancer, about a year apart, that they began chatting on the phone more often. The cashew conversation was one of many unusual offshoots of their "cancer connection."

Another was the strange spectacle of the two of them, hairless and beardless following chemotherapy. I had never seen either my husband or Gene without a full beard, and it was a surreal experience for the whole family. We endeavored to keep things as positive as we could (my daughter, for example, noted that their new hair, as it grew in, felt as soft as bunny fur), but it was a most difficult time for all of us.

When Phil was diagnosed, just over a year before Gene, I was able, somehow, to tell my children and close friends the news. But I simply couldn't tell Phil's parents. It was all I could do to call Gene and his wife, Joyce, knowing my words would cause them pain, to ask if they would go to Mom and Dad and tell them.

Ironically, little more than a year later, Phil and I were with his parents when we learned that Gene, too, had cancer. Hearing this news, I couldn't believe the unfairness of it. Why, I asked God, should they *both* have cancer? Why?

The worst part of it was having to watch my elderly in-laws, two kind and gentle people whom I love, dealing with the pain of seeing two of their three children struggling against cancer. Given the choice, I would cheerfully have walked on hot coals or chewed ten-penny nails—anything—if it would have spared Mom and Dad such pain. And of course, they themselves would have gladly, so gladly, taken the place of their boys, if only they could.

It has been eight years now since Gene passed away. Even after so long, I find I am struggling with tears as I write this. I am trying to remember what the positives were, the silver linings that got us all through that dark time.

One blessing, as Gene often said himself, was that he had had a good life, all the way up to that final year. He had worked hard, enjoyed a long and happy marriage, and raised a son, Kevin, who was the apple of his eye. He also was a devoted son, brother and uncle, and had a couple of years to savor his first grandchild, Kyle, before the illness. And Kyle's little sister, Katie, arrived a few weeks after Gene's death, bringing hope and new life to us.

Another compensation during this time of Phil's illness and the loss of Gene was that we all seemed to draw closer together as a family. I have felt an extra closeness to Phil's sister, Sharyn, since then; Gene's wife, Joyce, and I developed a strong bond, since both of our husbands had cancer. A year or two after Gene's death (actually, Joyce called him by his first name, "Kenny," while the rest of us called him by his middle name), Joyce said something to me that I've never forgotten. She said that if one of the brothers had to go, it was perhaps better that it was Kenny, since their child, Kevin, was grown up, and our Andrew was still so small. Such a breathtakingly generous comment; it helped allay some of the irrational guilt I felt that Phil had survived, while Gene, sadly, had not.

After Phil was diagnosed, Gene, ever the elder brother, had protectively watched over him. Gene flinched when watching Phil inch his way down the steps after back surgery. He would call and suggest we *not* come to family gatherings, because he worried that Phil wasn't up to it. He carried our son, Andrew, on his shoulders as we walked in the woods. Even after he died, Gene gave Phil one last message of encouragement, in the form of a dream.

Several months after Gene's death, Phil dreamed that he had been somewhere with Gene, perhaps at a holiday dinner at Mom and Dad's. He knew that this didn't make sense, because Gene had died. Somehow, though, in the dream Phil was driving his brother home (back to heaven?).

As they drove along, they encountered a huge pile of dirt in the middle of the road, covering both lanes and even the ditches. Phil decided to drive up it, but soon had to stop; it was so steep, the car almost tipped over backwards. So, he backed down the hill. With so many obstacles, he wondered, how would he get Gene back to heaven?

Next scene: Phil was still driving, with Gene alongside him. He asked Gene what heaven was like. Gene's response seemed to be, "Closed, Phil. Heaven is closed." At first, he took this to mean that Gene, always a man of few words, wasn't going to answer the question. Eventually, Phil gathered that his brother was saying, "You don't need to know right now. That information is available only at the appropriate time for each person."

Phil took great comfort in this. It seemed to him that his older brother was still looking out for him, that he was saying, "You don't need to worry, Phil. It's not your time." And Gene, as it turned out, was right.

Because he hated to say goodbye, Gene always said "See ya" instead. We could hardly bear to say goodbye to you, Gene dear, but someday, we hope, we'll see you.

Third Stop:

The Lemonade Stand

It's hard to get a glimpse inside the boarded-up window of the lemonade stand, but we can just make out the old-fashioned juicer standing ready on the counter. Have you ever stopped to think that, though lemons are so sour, adding a little sugar turns them into the most delicious lemonade? Are you getting the message? Add something good to everything that happens in your life. You can't control the circumstances, but sometimes you can sweeten them up.

*   *   *

"Don't Forget Vince!"

During the early years of his illness, Phil was hospitalized seemingly forever—fourteen times in the first year, and many times since then. Sometimes we knew he was going in; often it has been unexpected. But, either way, there is always a dark and painful silence, as we pack his bag. This is one aspect of the illness that has not gotten easier with time; it continues to be a difficult moment for us both. Phil is often in denial, especially if he's not feeling well, and tries to convince me that he doesn't need to go. I don't relish my role as "the heavy," insisting that we have to go, so I try hard to hide my feelings, the ache of unshed tears in my throat, by being brisk and upbeat, saying things like, "Well, they may not need to keep you. We might be coming right back home." It doesn't help much.

What does help is Vince. He is the lifeline, the bridge between hospital and home, a friend who makes the moment of truth more palatable. Dressed in chic, shiny silver battle attire, complete with a tiny shield, helmet, sword and sandals, Vince wears a perpetually hopeful smile on his crinkled, beige face. His bright-yellow hair stands wildly on end. His beady brown eyes seem to say, "It'll be o.k. I'm here!"

"Vince" is short for "Invincible," a reminder of the spirit we've tried to have about the illness. Given to Phil by a friend soon after diagnosis, Vince has faithfully served us ever since. Visitors who notice Vince see merely a cute little troll doll with crazy yellow hair, but to us Vince is far more than that. He has gone to the hospital each time, and has brightened up Phil's room, but Vince's true mission, his highest calling, has been to lighten that painful moment in the bedroom when we have to pack Phil's bag. For that, we are eternally grateful. We salute you, Vince dear!

Rosalie's Christmas

One of the most valuable lessons I've learned from the cancer journey is how much life there is to be embraced, even (perhaps especially) in the face of death. Over the years, a few people have asked me how I can stand the "downer" of spending time with people who are dying. They ask why I surround myself with people who are in the throes of dealing with a loved one's serious illness. They suggest that Phil and I go to too many funerals, buy too many get well cards, and spend too much time listening to stories of pain and suffering. They say that, since my husband is ill, it might be better for us to seek out "healthy" people, to counteract the heartache we carry with us daily.

I'm sure these people mean well, but sometimes I feel like screaming, "These people are *YOU!* They are *ME!* Death and illness are part of the fabric of life—not the opposite of life!" Abandoning folks who are in pain would be tantamount to abandoning oneself. Everyone, after all, is in the same boat. It's just that some of us don't realize it yet.

Additionally, there is such comfort in sharing the journey with those who understand, those who've been down that same frightening, unmarked road. It's similar to the bond that old soldiers share with their wartime comrades. Or the closeness team members share, years after a historic victory on the gridiron. Or the wordless joy that is transmitted from one spouse to the other, as they witness the birth of their firstborn child. We all feel deeply connected to those with whom we share meaningful passages in our lives.

Cancer has given me the opportunity to know some wonderful people (Janice, Ed, Mary Anne and Rosalie, this especially means you!) I would otherwise never have met. It is an honor to share such an intimate chapter in others' lives, and a comfort to have their help in facing my own bad moments. What a relief to be able to unburden oneself of the darkest, angriest, or most despairing thoughts, knowing that you are fully understood. How satisfying it is to feel that some stray word of mine may have helped to lighten someone else's burden, if only for a moment. What a blessing it is to pray together, trusting God for answers to questions we can't bear to ask, while holding on to each other like a lifeline.

I've never cried harder, or laughed more heartily, than with my "cancer buddies." No one loves life more, or embraces it more fully, than those who have grieved. No one is more courageous than those who must let their loved ones go, and then somehow make their way alone. I have learned so much about trust, faith, and courage from those with whom I've walked on this journey.

Here's a case in point. I got to know Rosalie at my cancer group. Her husband of some twenty years, Reed, had been diagnosed with lung cancer several months before and was now near death. With great courage, Rosie had struggled against the prognosis, searched for any glimmer of hope and finally, graciously, accepted it. She turned her attention from her own feelings of pain and loss to ensuring that Reed would have the fullest possible quality of life for as long as possible. Inch by inch, she retreated against the inevitable. Constantly surrendering precious bits and pieces of her life with Reed as his condition worsened, her dedication to him never flagged. Finally, she hoped for only one thing: that she and Reed could enjoy one last Christmas together.

It was not to be, however. Rosie called me one day, about a week before Christmas, to say that Reed had died. Knowing how much she had wanted just a few more precious days, I said, "Oh, Rosie, I'm so sorry you and Reed didn't get to have Christmas together, as you had hoped." Her response staggered me. She said, most enthusiastically, "But honey, we had Christmas! We just had it EARLY!"

I learned a valuable lesson from Rosie that day, about love, about life, about courage. I learned that it is possible to embrace death as heartily as one embraces life. I learned that death, no matter how unwelcome it may be, is nevertheless part of life. I learned that if one can find just one tiny drop of lemonade in a batch of bitter lemons, one can somehow survive the cruelest of losses. Thanks, Rosie.

Iron Bro

As a little boy, he was called "Robbie." In his teens, it was shortened to "Rob." Later, he began to use his middle name, "Brian," which is how he is universally known today. My kids, however, call him "Uncle Robert," often shortened to an affectionate "Unc." I still call him "Rob," just because someone should, though in our endless emails, I address him as "Row Bear," a takeoff on the French pronunciation of Robert. Here, just to make him happy, I will refer to him as "Brian," but no matter what you call him, he's my little brother . . . and a quite remarkable human being.

On September 11, 2001, as news of the terrorist attacks spewed forth from a television in a surgical waiting room, my sister and I recoiled in horror, both from the national disaster unfolding before us, and from the news that our brother had bladder cancer. Since then, he's had numerous surgeries and procedures, chemotherapy and many unexpected hospitalizations due to complications. Through it all, he's maintained his famous, wicked sense of humor, complaining very little about how lousy he was feeling physically, and barely at all about how much this event has challenged his emotions and forever changed his life.

Brian is a nurse. He has dedicated his life, both at work and personally, to caring for and about others. His career choices reveal much about him: he worked for many years in the emergency room of a city hospital. He also served as an angel of mercy to countless AIDS patients, some of whom were his friends. Through the strength of his love and his meticulous nursing care, he helped a friend adjust to a new life when she became a quadriplegic. Following a stint at a correctional facility, where he cared for some of the state's most dangerous criminals, Brian worked at an inner city mental health clinic, where he ministered to homeless people.

Because he has way too much nervous energy, Brian has always found therapy in keeping his hands busy. He is never without a computer mouse in hand, unless he puts it down long enough to crochet sweaters, hats, scarves and potholders. During the long recovery period, he's whipped out several gorgeous sweaters (though not, so far, hint, hint, one for me). He also, I kid you not, spins his own yarn.

Speaking of spinning yarns, my brother is also a talented writer, with a style both humorous and poignant. I cherish his hysterically funny emails, on topics ranging from social justice issues and politics to detailed descriptions of life in the ER. He's also begun his first book, hospital stories that express the laughter, joys and sorrows found in moments of illness and grief.

Please don't get to thinking of this man as a candidate for sainthood, however. He definitely has faults—not wanting to talk to his sister on the phone when she's worried about him, for one, and occasional displays of an insufferable, smart-mouth attitude, for another. He is often irreverent, somewhat distant at times, and has the usual array of annoying family quirks—none of which disguises the caring and courage that are his trademark qualities.

For example, when Brian was waiting to be admitted to the hospital once, due to yet another nasty infection, he emailed me that there was no available room, so he would have to wait for someone to either "go home or catch the Jesus Train." (This reminds me of another of his naughty medical terms: "circling the drain," or "CTD," which refers to one who is near death.)

When he first described the complicated surgery he would have to undergo, he referred to it as "a delightful procedure." He informed us of the results of a lung x-ray by saying: "The chest x-ray was clear; a relief to me, if to no one else." Just before the lengthy and difficult surgery to remove his bladder and prostate, Brian mentioned to a friend that he hoped the tumor was large enough that he would "emerge from surgery with a 32-inch waist." He also referred to the extremely large incision as "another charming feature of the surgery."

The greatest testament to my brother's impact on the world is the support he's received from his legion of friends since diagnosis. All through this ordeal, his wonderful friends have taken turns staying overnight with him, either at home or at the hospital. They've changed dressings, administered meds—whatever was needed. When Brian came home from surgery, his friend Nando moved in to provide round-the-clock care. His coworkers donated over 100 hours of their own sick time for his use. In the hospital, he had an endless stream of visitors who kept him company, ran errands and kept his spirits up. Brian's friends are exceptional, but they would tell you it's because he's such an exceptional friend himself.

Though I see him as a person of great faith, Brian says he really doesn't believe in God. That's okay with me, because the God I believe in, a being of love, joy and peace, so obviously inhabits my brother's kind heart and tender soul.

Recently, I gave Brian another nickname, one that came to me when I saw how unsinkable he is, how he gets up after every setback, dusts himself off, and heads back to the business of life. It came to me when I saw that, even though I'm the big sister, Brian is my teacher. I love you, Iron Bro.

Fly Me to the Moon

It's just a tiny framed print, about 4" x 6" in size, but it has loomed large in the Myeloma Saga over the years. It was a greeting card that I spied at Pier 1—an inexpensive decorating touch, I thought. So I framed it and hung it by the phone in the kitchen. It's all in green and gold and white. It features a large, whimsical insect, flying towards a distant crescent moon. At the bottom of the print, in small letters, are the words "fly me to the moon."

I cannot tell you how many times I've glanced at this little print, usually while dialing the phone. Not simply dialing—but often *frantically* dialing the oncologist's office or the hospital . . . or various and sundry relatives and friends who need to be informed whenever I've dialed the oncologist or the hospital.

Sometimes, my response when eyeing this picture is directed at the bug, flying perpetually towards that distant moon: "Take me with you, little buddy, please!" Or: "Give me a lift, Bug. I'm not heavy, I'm your sister!" Other times I ignore the bug and focus on the words instead. At such moments, my true creativity emerges, as I direct various thoughts (sometimes aloud) to the Deity: "Yes, God, that's a great idea! Please fly me to the moon—NOW!" Or: "Fly me, Baby, right outta here! I am *sooo* ready!"

I'm chuckling as I write this, because I bet you thought cancer's worst effects happen to the person diagnosed with it. Certainly that's true overall, but in "Myeloma Land" there is a little-known side effect—insanity—that's often seen in the patient's family members. Sometimes it takes the form of talking to bug pictures. Ha, ha! Ha, ha! (maniacal laughter is heard, fading gradually away. . . .)

A Little Bit of Heaven

It was modestly packaged in a white plastic refrigerator container. Opening it, I felt my heart turn over with sheer joy. Oh, the comfort of it! The beauty! The healing, restorative, qualities it represented! A riot of colors presented itself to me as I removed the lid— orange, green, yellow, white, and brown—all dancing together in a radiant swirl of iridescent liquid. It was love. It was life. It was strength. It was hope, at a time when it was sorely needed. It was . . . my mother-in-law's homemade vegetable soup.

An "Almost Oprah" Experience

Several years ago, I received a phone call, out of the blue, that absolutely floored me. Most people would say it was the call of a lifetime. I had to ask my caller, Kathy Lamancusa, to repeat what she had said, because I couldn't believe it. What she said was, "Would you like to be taped to appear on *The Oprah Winfrey Show?*" Kathy added that my husband, Phil, and our young son, Andrew, were also to appear on the show.

Numbly, I grabbed my appointment book and went through the motions of seeing if we were free at the appointed time, two days away. Then I began to laugh hysterically, at the thought that *anything* on my schedule could possibly be more important. So, even though there wasn't time for me to lose 20 pounds, I quickly said yes.

Believe it or not, my excitement was *not* because I'm a fan of Oprah's show. I'm not much into TV, so I had never even seen it . . . something that caused most people to whom I mentioned this fact to stare at me as if I had suddenly, right before their eyes, transmogrified into a chartreuse and purple critter from outer space. Nevertheless, I hasten to add that I *am* a major Oprah fan, but it's because of her excellent magazine, which I read eagerly, cover-to-cover, each month. So yes, I was pumped!

Oh, you want to know why we were taped for Oprah's show? I had written a story called "Daddy's Tree," about our family's struggle with my husband's illness (multiple myeloma). It appeared in Kathy Lamancusa's book, *Flowers Are Forever*, which had just been published by Simon & Schuster. The producer had seen an excerpt and was sending a camera crew to Canton, Ohio, where Kathy resides, to tape her there. Kathy, in turn, invited us (along with two other local contributors to her book) to come and be taped.

Though we felt rather self-conscious in the presence of the camera, once we got into our stories the taping was really fun. They taped Phil and Andrew playing football, and I was interviewed by the producer, who asked questions about "Daddy's Tree," and about what our life was like, living with an incurable illness.

Eventually, we learned when the segment would air. Euphoria reigned. Word spread like wildfire among my business associates and friends that we were going to be on *Oprah*. It even got mentioned in two local papers. Suddenly, I had a tiny inkling of what it must be like to be Oprah, living with all this uproar around her, and I thought: "Girlfriend, you have my sympathy, because this is like living in the proverbial fishbowl!"

The big day finally arrived and we sat in the den, glued to the television. We learned, among other things, how to duct tape our breasts to enhance cleavage. (I heard later that this segment was particularly enlightening for my 90-year-old aunt, who happens to be a nun.) Finally, at the end of the show, Kathy Lamancusa and the other contributors to her book appeared onscreen—everyone except Phil, Andrew and me. Suddenly, the credits were rolling; the show was over and our segment, it became obvious, had been left on the cutting room floor.

At first, I felt sick to my stomach, embarrassed that so many friends and colleagues were watching the show on my behalf . . . and I was a no show. I somehow felt that I had let them down. When I thought about how much our segment would have helped to raise awareness about multiple myeloma, I felt even worse. Then, a Bible verse, one rather unfamiliar to me, suddenly popped into my mind: "I will lift up my eyes to the hills, from whence comes my help."

Taking a deep breath, I realized that I needed to "lift up" my consciousness about what had happened. I needed to "head for the hills" in my thinking, rather than feeling downcast. I realized that the purpose of our being taped for the show hadn't been what it seemed; it wasn't about being on TV at all. And I experienced great peace, as I got the real message.

Being taped for the show gave me a chance to relive the earliest, ugliest days of Phil's illness, and to recognize how far we had come since those dark times. Watching Phil and Andrew tossing the football for the camera gave me a chance to realize what riches my life contained. I saw that what mattered was that Phil was still alive. What first seemed disappointing actually created an avenue by which I could experience increased gratitude for my circumstances. The hubbub surrounding being on TV would have distracted me from appreciating this precious gift.

So, as I told an audience of 150 business people the next day, the outpouring of support and caring from others, and the chance to re-count our blessings, were wonderful gifts we received from our almost Oprah Experience.

As far as being on the show, all I can say is, Oprah may have missed an opportunity, but I missed nothing at all, thanks to the wisdom of the Producer Upstairs, who knew exactly what was best for me.

A Tribute to Ann Landers

Dear Margo:

Please accept my heartfelt sympathy in the recent loss of your dear mother, known to the world as Ann Landers. I know that your loss is profound, and personal. But, like millions of other people who knew your mom through her column, I grieve her passing too. I didn't know her as you did, of course. I have no idea what little foibles or flaws she might have had, what she liked to eat for dinner, how she spent her free time. But somehow, through the strange alchemy that is love, that is caring, that was your mother's special grace, I have always felt connected to her and now, to you, because I know what it is to lose one's beloved mother.

Though your mother was a Jewish lady and mine was Italian Catholic, they shared much in common: they were both Midwest girls; they were just a few years apart in age, they were both "vertically challenged," and they were both concerned for the needs of others. I believe, too, that they shared an unsinkable spirit, a common sense approach to the vicissitudes of life, and a wish to leave the world a better place than they found it.

I feel my mother changed the world, albeit in a modest way; and obviously yours did too—in ways far-reaching and lasting. You must be so proud of her. Her column's legacy has been secured, for all time. It's one of wit, wisdom and kindness. None of that will ever be lost, just as she herself can never truly be gone from us. Her spirit will shine through forever, from the thousands of dog-eared columns, yellowed with age, that her readers have clipped from newspapers over the years. Those favorite columns, so rich in wisdom that we couldn't bear to part with them, eventually found their way into wallets, Bibles, desk drawers—and who knows where else? Few individuals make such a loving and lasting impact on the world.

Your mother's impact on my life began in 1963, when I was thirteen years old. Reading her column became a daily ritual for me. I also met her once, at an event where she spoke. Like so many, I was always going to write to her, but never did. Yet I learned so much from her: how to survive the trials and tribulations of the teen years, how to live honestly and with integrity, how to make better decisions. I received an education in how others lived, how much pain there is in the world, how much more alike we are than different, and how rewarding it can be to make those difficult but necessary personal changes.

Her ability to call things as she saw them, along with her humility and her willingness to say she was wrong (though I think readers were often too hard on her; didn't their mothers teach them not to be rude?) helped me to aspire to those qualities. Your mom's wisdom and humor helped me as a young bride, a harried mother, a young divorcee, a second-time bride. She taught me how to let go of my children once they were grown, so they could go off and make lives of their own. And yes, I learned that there is more than one way to hang a roll of toilet paper.

Most of all, though, your mother inspired me to write. From the time I was a teenager, I dreamed of having a syndicated column, because she made it seem possible. I remember asking my mother what "syndicated" meant; I thought it was a wondrous thing. I haven't quite made it yet, but I am so grateful to have learned, from your mother's example, to follow my dreams.

Like my mom, your mother always had one more thing to tell me. I only wish she had said it while I could still respond to her. You see, my husband has multiple myeloma. He was diagnosed over nine years ago, and is doing well. I always planned to write to your mother about it, because I knew she would help me tell the world about this disease. That's just how she was—always willing to help, always compassionate. But when I learned she herself had myeloma, I was so sad. If only I had known, maybe I could have given her some comfort or encouragement, as she had always given me. I would have prayed for her, and perhaps made her laugh. It would have been a very personal bond to share with one who had given so much to me. But I'd be the first to defend her right to privacy. In death, as in life, she showed us how to be true to ourselves.

I hope it comforts you, Margo, to know that, in some small way, you have legions of sisters and brothers who grieve with you, and who will live and love a bit more successfully for having known your mother. Thank you for sharing her with us.

Fourth Stop:

Laugh Tracks

Feeling a bit better? As you glance inside the window of this deserted arcade, you can almost hear the laughter echoing inside. It's clear that kids of all ages have had a great time here. The dusty games you see inside remind you of innocence and joy—your own innocence and joy. Can you remember how, as a child, when you were afraid, or when you skinned your knee, laughter soon returned, banishing the tears? Do you realize that, even today, laughter can help you heal? Some moments, of course, are just too hard to smile our way through. But sometimes laughter truly is the best medicine.

*   *   *

A Big Fat Italian Funeral

I finally had a chance to see *My Big Fat Greek Wedding*, the relatively low-budget film that somehow has defied the odds and become a big hit. I not only saw the movie, but in a way I actually lived it for a couple of days.

I do not, at least as far as I know, possess even a smidgen of Greek heritage. However, as anyone who has seen *Greek Wedding* will tell you, part of its charm is that, regardless of your ethnic background, as long as your family is stubborn, contentious and opinionated, you'll relate to the characters and situations portrayed. I am Italian. Any questions?

So, when I was in Columbus recently, my brother, Brian, and I went to see the movie. As the saga unfolded, I laughed uproariously because, as outrageous as the characters were, they seemed strangely familiar. The movie also made me cry because, compared to these characters' robust lives, my own seemed lackluster, a pallid black-and-white existence.

That reaction, though, was partly because we had just come from a funeral, and I was worn out. You see, the real story here isn't a big fat Greek wedding, but a big fat Italian funeral. Just prior to seeing the movie, I had spent a day and a half with my large, vibrant, opinionated Italian family (are you catching my drift?), for my aunt's wake and funeral.

Aunt Clara, who was 98, was the feistiest of all Mom's siblings, a quality she retained until the end. I remember the last family funeral, about a year ago. At that time, Aunt Clara was becoming just a bit forgetful. But you could never discount her as some little old lady sitting in a corner. She was still very much present.

After the funeral that day, an elderly man hobbled up to Aunt Clara and whispered something in her ear. Obviously, there was nothing wrong with her hearing. She pushed him away, laughing, arching an eyebrow flirtatiously in his direction. I was stunned to realize (child that I am, still learning from my elders) that, at 97, she was still very much a woman.

One of Mom's other sisters, Aunt Mildred, died recently too, at 94. She was intensely alive, like all the rest, but not quite as naughty as Aunt Clara. (Then again, a woman who writes letters on toilet paper is not exactly sedate.) What I remember about Aunt Mil is that she was always laughing. No matter what life brought her, she found humor in it. She even drew little smiley faces on her cards and letters, at random intervals, to make us laugh.

But, I digress. Back to Aunt Clara's funeral. My oldest first cousin is 82; the youngest of us, at 47, is my brother. There are more than 100 second, third and maybe fourth cousins, many of whom were at the calling hours. The room wasn't big enough to hold all those personalities—those who were barely speaking; those who were speaking and you wished they would shut up; those who said how lovely someone looked, though you knew they were lying through their teeth; and those who simply smiled and hugged.

The energy level was titanic; the high-volume laughter, tears, and talking, the love, concern and warmth. It was so overwhelming that I felt a bit dizzy at times. It was like watching a play . . . or that Greek wedding movie.

Here's one scene: When Aunt Louise, Mom's youngest remaining sister (93), who happens to be a nun, inched her way into the funeral home on her walker, one of my cousins (age 70-ish) shouted, quite disrespectfully, I thought: "There's no room at the inn!" Instead of being shocked, my aunt grinned from ear to ear. She loved it. I suspect Paul has been needling Aunt Louise since he was old enough to talk, and I suspect he learned it from her.

People from every generation kept a watchful and protective eye over the two elderly aunts who were present. (Believe it or not, there are still two others, even older, who were not there.) When Aunt Louise began to cry at one point, a blizzard of Kleenexes appeared, as everyone rushed to her, nearly suffocating her with hugs and kisses. Then, when her tears subsided, everyone went back to discussing who "really looks old," etc.

There is something quite magnificent about the passion and energy of such a large family. I am so proud of them, even though it wears me out to be with them. And it is comforting, somehow, to know that I am theirs and they are mine. Many of us barely know each other, yet we are inextricably connected. In each other's hair, eyes, body shapes and attitudes we see the past, and the future. We are family. It's mysterious, to say the least. In fact, it's all Greek to me.

"He Just Won't Die!"

A number of years ago, perhaps two or three years into Phil's illness, we were gathered around the table, ready to celebrate Thanksgiving. Our immediate family—Phil, Jay, Mike, Kerry, Andrew and I—along with my brother, Brian, were present. We had passed the turkey, gravy, dressing, mashed potatoes, rolls and assorted vegetables, and it was time to say grace before the meal. I suggested that, in lieu of a formal prayer, we each simply share something for which we were thankful. I don't recall what the rest of us mentioned, but I'm quite sure none of us will ever forget my daughter's comment. When it was her turn, Kerry blurted out, "I'm thankful Phil is still here. (Pause.) He just won't die!"

There was dead silence. Everyone looked at Phil, then at me, then at each other. After a moment, I began to laugh, soon followed by Phil, and then by the kids and Brian. This may seem shocking to you, since there is such a mystique around cancer. On television, for example, no one ever makes an irreverent remark about (or to) someone with an incurable illness. There are no jokes, there is no teasing . . . cancer is serious business!

Now of course there *are* moments that demand seriousness. There are people who would be hurt or could misunderstand lighthearted remarks about cancer. I would never condone hurting another person's feelings, or making light of a serious situation. However, humor has always been a strong part of my family's tradition, as has candor.

Our family could never be accused of being like the adorable—
and adoring—families in greeting card commercials. We do not
gaze lovingly at each other, our eyes softening at the pure joy of
being part of the same family. We do not pause respectfully when
someone else reaches for the turkey, deferring lovingly to our
sibling or spouse. Instead, we snatch another serving for ourselves
as the platter goes by. We bug each other constantly. We argue
about meaningless details. We helpfully point out each other's
flaws. We are opinionated, intense, irreverent.

But these same qualities are the very ones that were missing
during the first part of Phil's illness. We were grieving. We couldn't
joke about cancer, because it was too big in our lives. We couldn't
tease Phil; it didn't seem right. So, when Kerry made her blunt
Thanksgiving comment, I was relieved; in fact, all of us were, I
think. Because the fact that Kerry, who loves her stepfather very
much, could say such a thing meant to me that we were finding
ways to make cancer a smaller part of our lives. We were learning
to put cancer in its place. And it gave us a chance to feel a rush
of gratitude, a moment of absolute joy, as we savored this
holiday . . . *together.*

Find the Humor In Everything

I take seriously the concept of *not* taking life too seriously. Life works best and is most enjoyable to me—no matter what is going on—if I can find humor in everything . . . and I do mean "everything."

One of my favorite forms of humor is irreverence. It's a sort of an inner grin that I get when others seem to take life too seriously.

It's time for that inner grin, as far as I'm concerned, when I encounter people whose lives are completely planned. You know who these people are. While you're trying to decide how you're going to manage your next 10 minutes, they've got their entire year planned, right down to the second.

They tell you, quite blithely, what they'll be doing six months from now—and they're serious about it! They really think they can plan that far ahead. "On October 12th of next year, we'll pick up our brand-new Lexus and drive it—in 6.2 hours exactly—to Cape Cod. We'll arrive at 6:22 p.m., pull into the La-Di-Da Seafood Restaurant, and order dinner." And then, they add the kicker: "I will have the scrod, while Mildred will order filet mignon . . ."

I have to chuckle about people like this, to avoid going crazy. I simply can't deal with this mentality, especially since my own life has been anything but predictable. I want to scream, "Get real! No one knows what they'll be doing at 6:22 p.m. on October

12th, and it's probably better that way!" My irreverent inner grin is invaluable at such moments, usually keeping me from blurting out such rude comments. I try instead to say, politely, "Oh, I'm sure that will be fun."

It's also important to be able to laugh at oneself. Here's an example:

What do you do when you're stuck in traffic on the expressway? You're going to be late for an appointment with a new client . . . and your cell phone is out of juice, so you can't even call to say you'll be late.

I have heard that there are people who can remain calm at such times. They turn on the radio, dust off the dashboard, clean out the glove box, etc. I truly envy people who are so grown up, who are able to deal maturely with this situation. Unfortunately, I am not one of them.

What I usually do is . . . throw a fit. Embarrassing but true. I try to be good, I really do. But before you know it, I'm acting like Donald Duck. Squawk, squawk, squawk! I'm sure this is quite entertaining to the people around me. Gives them something to focus on while they're cleaning out their cup holders and tidying up their briefcases.

But after acting like an idiot, I get a mental picture of myself and then I just have to laugh. I wish I could laugh first, and ixnay the fit throwing. But I know I will do it again, next time I'm stuck in traffic, even though I will end up feeling like a fool (again). So I have to laugh at myself!

Is it possible to laugh about more serious matters—even illness, divorce, death? I say *yes!* Of course, none of these situations is intrinsically funny. Illness, death, divorce and other painful circumstances hurt people, and there's nothing at all humorous about that. But I believe that, at the right moment, even serious situations can contain humor. Taking a humorous approach, I find, keeps me from feeling like a victim. Here's an example:

Have you ever been diagnosed with "atypical" cells or some other weird ailment following a checkup? I have. In fact, I've been "atypical" for a number of years now, according to my gynecologist. Here is how I choose to think about it:

"Wow. Atypical cells. I've never had those before. It sounds a bit scary, especially since my husband already has cancer. What will happen to our son, if I have cancer too? But wait a minute. The doctor doesn't sound too concerned, so maybe I don't need to be either. Atypical cells. You know, I'm thinking this is kind of neat! Not everyone has atypical cells. Most people just have the regular, everyday variety. But I'm an over-achiever. I've got atypical, *special* cells! I'm not "normal," I'm actually quite cool. Why would I want to settle for ordinary?"

Now maybe I'm a fool, but this is my way of controlling my own destiny. I hasten to add that I don't ignore reality. You'd better believe I'm on my doctor's doorstep every six months for my checkup. But I decided that I was not going to invest much energy in worrying about this. Whatever may happen years from now— both good and bad—has not happened yet. Why would I want to waste my precious time worrying about cancer cells that may never show up?

By the way, after several years I finally had two checkups in a row that showed only normal cells. I thought I was through with seeing my doctor every six months. But after the third checkup, the nurse called and said, "Guess what? They're baaaaack . . . and we need to see you in six months." My response: "Would you please tell Alan (that's my doctor) that we could have coffee or something. We don't *have* to keep meeting this way!" But they wouldn't listen, so the checkups continued until, eventually, my "super cells" reverted to "normal."

The point is, laugh whenever you can. And you almost always can. Whatever happens in life, try to see the lighter side. It's good for your blood pressure. And it keeps you out of Adversity Plaza.

Try A Little "Tweeziness"

I don't know how much more of this I can take. The days are shorter, but my "to do" list isn't; the days are darker and colder, just when I need sunshine and warmth. Every day between now and Christmas is spoken for, as a workday or a shopping day. Everyone wants a piece of my time, but I feel like giving them a piece of my mind. Nothing goes smoothly; everything is a hassle.

A case in point: the other evening, two of my friends were coming over for a simple, "just us girls" soup and salad dinner. I didn't obsess much about how the house looked, but I did decide to spruce up my messy office and organize some of the many books that reside in the den. Sounds simple, right? Hah!

First, I discovered that we had no napkins. Deciding it would be simpler to go buy some than to (horrors!) iron actual cloth napkins, I headed to the nearest grocery store. On the way, reflecting on my soon-to-arrive guests, one of whom is my bookkeeper and the other my CPA, I realized, to my dismay, that I hadn't written my quarterly tax checks, which were due in 48 hours. So I ran back home, wrote the checks and stuffed them in the envelopes. I grabbed the napkins and came home, only to realize that we were almost out of milk. My son's bones may stop growing because of this lack of calcium, but I just couldn't drag myself back to the store. He's already well over four feet tall, so how tragic can this be?

Back home, I discovered, after organizing an entire row of books nicely on a shelf, that I had put some of the shelves too close together. I figured this out, of course, only as I tried to shelve the very last book, which was a hair taller than the rest, and wouldn't fit. So, I decided to file awhile in my office instead. The more I filed, the more I realized how much more there was to be filed. It was so discouraging that I decided instead to just tidy up the piles. Bad idea. The resulting avalanche made an even worse mess.

I bolted my office door shut and decided I would tell my guests that my son, Andrew, had accidentally super-glued it, so they would understand why they couldn't venture in there. (Actually, this would be a great way to get a day off work—just super-glue the office door and I'm free. But, I digress.)

Next, after shooing my husband and son out the door for a burger and basketball practice, I tried for five minutes to open a jar of salsa that simply wouldn't budge. I was tempted to take a hammer to it, but thought that eating glass particles might be a turnoff to my friends. Instead, I decided to make opening the jar into a competition, to see which of my guests could open it first. The winner would get . . . first dibs on the salsa.

I glanced at my son's goldfish tank as I struggled with the salsa jar. One of the fish, a very pudgy little critter, stared back at me, quite critically, I felt. I just knew he was thinking, "Boy, is *she* a grouch! And she can't even open the salsa!" He's lucky I didn't pluck him out of the water to serve as an appetizer.

I think you get the picture. I was in a very foul mood. I needed an attitude adjustment, a place to hide . . . comfort. Do you remember that wonderfully warm, cozy cuddling that Mom used to provide? That's what I needed; something to make me relax all the way down to "aaaahhhhh."

What comforts you, when you need it most? What do you do when you reach that "stop the world, I want to get off" point? A massage, TV, a manicure, a hug? Piles of lovely junk food, the sports channel, a good book (or a naughty one) and a couple of soft pillows? Primal scream therapy? Wine (or whining)?

I've tried most of the above, at various times. After much experimentation, I've devised the perfect plan. First, I visualize myself using a small pair of tweezers to delicately tweeze up all the people, things and situations that are bugging me. Next, I picture myself approaching the edge of a cliff, where I "un-tweeze" all of the annoyances, quite gently, and watch them fly away, down and down, until they become invisible specks in the distance. Then I smile, peacefully.

Next, I put on my oldest, grubbiest pair of p.j.'s, grab a book, and retire to my little retreat, a corner of my bedroom that is strictly off-limits to others. I curl up in my special chair, put my feet up on the ottoman, and snuggle into an afghan. Sometimes, if they're in a civil mood (and if they weren't among the aforementioned casualties tweezed off the cliff), I invite one of my cats to join me. Then, as I sink into the comfort of my chair, I let out a very deep breath. At some much later point, I rejoin the world, refreshed. But I take my tweezers along, just in case.

Lighten Up!

It was so funny that I laughed until I cried. As I re-read it, reclining on my satin bedspread, I nearly slid right off the bed, still laughing uproariously. My husband, meanwhile, looked at me as though I had (finally) lost my mind.

What was I reading that was so hilarious? It was a passage in a book, *Traveling Mercies*, that dealt with a point in author Anne Lamott's life in which she was coming to terms with her aging body. She had arrived at a point of acceptance. She could view the wrinkles, lumps, and somewhat faded beauty of her middle-aged body as a beloved testimony to her life. The imperfections, finally, could be seen as friends, as a badge of maturity, rather than as a negative mark of middle age.

She was doing just fine. In fact, she had gone walking on the beach without wearing a cover-up over her swimsuit—tremendous progress in her attitude, she felt. But suddenly something happened. Four teenage girls, young, slim and lovely, began walking towards her on the beach. It was her description of them that set me off. She said they emerged from the mist like "dogs from hell." I am laughing again as I write this, though you may be scratching your head, wondering what was so darn funny. Maybe you would need to read the entire chapter of the book to "get it." Or maybe you never would, since humor is such an individual thing. Different strokes for different folks.

The point is I think we all take life too seriously. We hesitate to laugh (is it politically correct . . . or not?), even when we *know* something is funny. We are uncertain about inserting humor into business situations, for fear of sending the wrong message. We worry that we won't (gasp!) be taken seriously if we are too humorous.

Of course, we must use common sense in determining when to use nonsense. We don't want to offend others. We don't want to make light of serious situations. But research has proven, again and again, that laughter is healthy. It is a fact that stressful situations, sad times, and even serious illnesses can be improved with humor. It is a fact that our energy level is improved, our attitude is brighter and life is easier when we laugh. And yet we hesitate to express the joy that lurks within.

A case in point: A man enters a sales office, banging the door back against the wall. He walks up to the startled receptionist, snarling: "I'm here about the sales job that was advertised!" When the sales manager approaches, the visitor grabs him by the lapels and roars, "You wanted someone who's aggressive. Is *THIS* aggressive enough for you?"

Oh, come on. Don't be uptight. Don't be horrified. This isn't a scary story from the evening news. There's no need to call the police to contain an explosive workplace situation. It didn't even happen! It's merely a frustrated job hunter's humorous fantasy, in response to reading too many job ads that all said the same thing.

Here's another story. A priest was attending a religious education workshop, along with 30 or 40 other people. The other people didn't know him well, but they did know he was a priest. Suddenly, he got the giggles. And couldn't seem to stop. The woman next to him, to whom he confided the source of his laughter, first laughed with him, then quickly stopped, in deference to the speaker. The woman urged the priest to pull himself together. "Will you *stop*," she whispered. "You're supposed to be setting an example!" The more she exhorted him to stop laughing, the more she reminded him that everyone was watching, the harder the priest laughed. Helpless to stop him, the woman drew her chair a bit away from his, as if to distance herself from his bad behavior.

Eventually, the priest regained control of his faculties. What was so funny? The speaker's shoes, which reminded him of shoes worn by nuns in the 1960's.

How you respond to that story speaks volumes about *you*, and the "humor quotient" in your life. Do you find it sacrilegious? Scandalous? Or do you find it refreshing . . . proof that priests, too, are (gasp!) "human"?

My point is that it is healthy—*necessary*—for us to laugh. It's good for our bodies . . . and for our spirits. And that's good for our work, our family, and our sanity! So start giggling!

Coffins, Wrinkles
and Integrity

My friend, Shirl, and I had an interesting conversation recently. It started out as a quick phone call to finalize dinner plans. We got into whether or not we'd opt for dessert with our meal. I said I planned, for caloric reasons, to have only a big salad. Shirl met this news with the comment, "Life is short, Kath; you can't give up all the fun stuff." My reply: "Yeah, life is short and I don't intend to lie in my coffin and have people say, "Too bad about Kathy. She never did lose that last ten pounds."

Shirl then pointed out, quite sensibly, that when I'm ensconced in my coffin, my stomach will be relatively flat, and I'll be tucked under an elegant satin blanket, guaranteed to gracefully disguise any extra tonnage. This seemed encouraging, so I began to reconsider my "no dessert" decision—until I became concerned that the blanket itself might add bulk, making me look fat despite my best efforts. My ever-practical friend said, "But what about the embalming process? I bet it works sort of like a diuretic, so we'd at least lose some fluid, wouldn't we?"

I wasn't buying it, even though I knew Shirl meant well. With dessert hanging in the balance (note to those who may not understand the female psyche: women don't eat dessert alone;

somehow, fewer calories settle on one's hips if one has a partner in crime), Shirl searched for inspiration.

"What about neon-bright orange nail polish?" she said. "It would definitely draw attention away from the flab." This was intriguing to me, because if I'm vain about anything, it's my hands. I bet I could have been a hand model. They're that nice. But my relief was short-lived. As I told Shirl, I don't look good in orange.

I don't remember whether we had dessert that night or not, but this conversation lingered in my mind. I thought about how hard we women are on ourselves, how we seldom feel slim enough, young enough, vibrant enough. It's no secret that we live in a society that values looks over substance and youth over wisdom, but what's sad is how automatically we buy into this unfair double standard, even when we should know better.

A case in point: both Barry Manilow and Carole King were on TV recently. As I turned on the tube and saw Barry, I thought, "He looks older! But of course that's to be expected, and he wears the wrinkles well." Flipping to another channel, I heard Carole King's still-excellent voice. My first thought was, "How could she appear on TV wearing a sleeveless shirt, at her age?" And how could I, as a fellow woman, feel so critical of her, simply for growing older?

Apparently, this obsession with looking young never ends. My 97-year-old aunt is still quite concerned about her appearance. It's nice that, when she feels up to it, she still gets a manicure, but why should she be agonizing at her age about a couple of stray chin hairs, or whether or not she looks "too old"? I know a lovely, gracious, still-vibrant lady who, though slim and trim, is dieting (at the age of 88) because she feels she's getting "a bit of a tummy."

So, I guess I have to accept that the obsession will never end. But, to combat it, and to convince myself I can still like my looks at any age, I've begun to clip out magazine photos of older women who look great. I've got a wonderful picture of Gloria Steinem at 66. Wearing her wrinkles proudly, with a "This is who I am, baby" expression, she faces the camera in her bare feet, wearing a velour tunic over stretch pants, with her long hair pulled back in a braid. I also have one of a sculptor, well into her 90's, whose graceful hands are buried in clay, and whose spirit is immersed in creativity . . . and life.

There is an intriguing woman I see at church who is obviously in her 70's, but whose attitude is about 15. She is petite, very attractive and quite eccentric, in both manner and conversation. She is always colorfully dressed and wears gobs of jewelry. On one recent Sunday, she was especially stunning, with rings on every finger, several necklaces, and a sparkling tiara, in addition to earrings and bracelets. (By now, you're probably wondering what church I attend.) Turns out the extra "glam" was in honor of her birthday. She had brought her own cake, asked someone to take a picture of her with it, and then led the singing of "Happy Birthday." What a gal!

Back to the coffin conversation: One of these days, I'll have to talk to my local funeral director, to find out if he offers any "super slimming" embalming techniques. I'll ask if we could possibly use a black satin blanket, instead of white, since I look good in black and it's *so* slimming. And here's a note to my children: When you make my arrangements, don't fuss about which casket to choose. I really don't care. Just make sure I look mighty fine in it.

Better yet, I'll make sure I live a mighty fine life, regardless of whether I'm fat or thin, wrinkly or smooth-skinned. I've decided that's all that really matters. So, please pass the dessert.

Send the Grinch

Back to Whoville

Virtually everyone has heard of the Grinch, Dr. Seuss' evil, churlish, nasty-natured bad boy, who topped his career of naughty no-no's by stealing . . . *Christmas!* He was rotten to the core. He was the meanest of the mean, the greenest of the green, the most crafty and cunning creature ever seen. His only enjoyment in life came from hurting others. He got up in the morning with a very short "to do" list. Apparently, all it said was, "Be mean today." And so he was.

Unfortunately, many of us know some real-life grinches. Worst of all, if we were being *perfectly* honest, we might even have to admit that (gasp!) we *ourselves* are sometimes somewhat grinchy. Not to worry. Grinch-like attitudes—our own or others'—*can* be cured.

When you think about it, that old Grinch was merely human . . . at least, as human as a Seuss character can be. His worst behavior was reserved for holiday time—a time that the rest of us, if we could just admit it, also find rather difficult. We want it to be perfect. We seek that moment in which all the relatives get along, the house looks lovely, the meals, the gifts, and the weather (just a little snow, please) are absolutely perfect, and where we adore every one of our family members, friends, co-workers, clients, and associates.

In reality, that's a pretty tall order. After all, even if you could completely control your own environment, mood and behavior (fat chance), you certainly cannot control everyone else's. And that is precisely when grinchiness begins.

Think about it: instead of a nice dusting of snow for Christmas Eve, you get buried under an unseasonable blizzard, a veritable avalanche of snow. So much of the white stuff falls, in fact, that you can't make it to Grandma's house for dinner.

Or, if you're the cook, instead of the exquisite, Martha Stewart-like holiday banquet you visualized, you end up burning the main course. You drop the gelatin on the kitchen floor. You forget to make ice. You cannot find the carving knife. Next, you discover (on the *only* day of the year when the stores are closed) that you don't have one of the key ingredients for the plum pudding. Not to mention the moment when your cousin, spying your beautiful *pièce de résistance*, shrieks, "I can't eat that! Don't you remember I'm allergic to kumquats?" It's enough to make a grown Whovillian cry.

And then there are the gifts, those perfect gifts that you lovingly spent hours and hours selecting and wrapping. Your daughter opens the gift you knew she wanted most—and sheepishly mentions that her boyfriend got her the same thing. As your brother-in-law opens his gift, the one you were *so sure* he would adore, you see on his face a look of utter dismay. A look that says, "How on earth could you think I'd like *this thing?*"

And you're so tired. And you've spent so much time and money on it all. And you begin to feel angry, annoyed, out of sorts, downcast, *GRINCHY!*

Please don't be so hard on yourself, binkie. It's not your fault everybody isn't satisfied. But I know a secret. There is a way to combat grinchiness—your own and everyone else's. Just sweeten things up with the twin weapons of eggnog (or other suitable holiday beverage, alcoholic or "non") and Christmas cookies. Add some false heartiness and you've got it made!

Heartiness really does help, if you can pull it off. The secret is to tell yourself over and over, like a mantra: "This, too, shall pass." Your wife informs you that her mother will be spending the next four nights at your house, instead of just the one night you had agreed to? You say, "Why, that's great, honey! The more the merrier!" Then take a sip of the ole' eggnog. Your four-year-old says, "I hate you!" in response to your every comment? No problem. Your hearty response is: "You do? I'm glad you're able to share your feelings with me, dear!" as you reach for a cookie. The neighbor's white cat takes a nap on your black coat while you're dropping off some mistletoe? No sweat. Just gush, as heartily as possible, "Oh, how nice! I always wanted a fur coat." Then head home to the eggnog and cookies.

The eggnog can be used offensively, as well as defensively. Your ex-husband plops down on the couch ("just to say hi to everyone") when he brings the kids home—while you're entertaining your new boyfriend and his family? Just say, "This is the kids' dad, Bill." Then, hospitably pour Bill some eggnog. *Lots* of eggnog. He'll soon be asleep . . . neutralized! You can now enjoy your other guests.

The eggnog-and-heartiness routine is helpful in the kitchen, too. It works wonders on your culinary skills, and makes others' holiday offerings palatable, too. For instance, if your aunt insists on bringing her special fruitcake, which you know is going to be as hard as a rock and similarly tasty, just baste it with eggnog to soften it up . . . or just baste yourself in eggnog. Same principle. Dropped your earring into the cookie batter? Not to worry. After another sip or two of eggnog, you'll be creative enough to turn it into a holiday festivity. Tell your guests that whoever finds the earring wins a prize!

And if all else fails, remember that the Grinch ends up being quite the jolly old green guy, in spite of himself. You'll make it, too. Just sit yourself down with the last glass of eggnog (spiked, at this point, would probably be best) and say, "Merry Christmas to me, and to everyone else . . . tough noogies!" Then, eat the rest of the cookies.

Free Ocean Vacation

Sometimes, the best thing you can do is cultivate the ability to laugh at yourself. Here's an example:

A few years ago, I had been yearning to go to the beach. But the budget wasn't cooperating, and I hadn't planned ahead, so it didn't seem possible that we could go. One day, however, a woman from my church called to ask if we'd like to spend a week with her, her husband, and a few of their friends at their beach house in North Carolina. She said our young son would be welcome too, and that we were to come as their guests.

Wow! The ocean. A beach-front house. For free! How would most people react to such a generous invitation? Probably start packing, right? But not me! I needed to think about it. In fact, I talked it over with God the next morning. (This illustrates not only my need to be able to laugh at myself, but also the fact that the Deity must have a sense of humor, to be able to deal with people like me.) So I said to God: "What should I do, Dear One?"

Suddenly, into my mind came a vision of an Old Testament-looking God, with a long white beard, smacking himself in the forehead in frustration, saying, "What am I going to do with you, Kathy? You want to go to the beach, and I give it to you . . . for a week! In a house right on the water! For FREE, no less! And you ask what you should do?" So, after having a belly laugh at my own expense, I gratefully accepted the offer and we went off to the beach.

Sometimes, to get the proper perspective on things, you just have to be able to step back and see how ridiculous you really are.

Fifth Stop:

The Little Chapel at the Plaza

This little storefront chapel has been empty for years, and yet it retains a luminous quality. Do you feel the glow of love, joy and peace that shine forth? Are you beginning to see that, no matter what happens in life, contentment is possible? Do you know that, somehow, there are always blessings to count? Do you realize that seeing them (or not) is a choice? Start counting.

*   *   *

Daddy's Tree

After my husband, Phil, was diagnosed with multiple myeloma, our life was forever changed. Some of the pieces of our old life remained, but couldn't be reassembled into their former pattern. Our life became an endless nightmare: tough decisions about treatment, endless days and nights of fear, pain and vigilance, constant worry about money, and tremendous grief and anger.

There was so much irony in this new life. Our baby's first steps paralleled Phil's careful steps following back surgery. In the hospital, we pushed Phil's wheel chair along in the hall next to Andrew's stroller. Our son played with real stethoscopes, borrowed from nurses, when he visited Daddy in the hospital, while other children played with toy doctor kits. Our son's laughter was beautiful to hear, but the flip side was our own tears of grief. Andrew's innocence and trust were in ugly juxtaposition to our loss of innocence, and to the wrenching uncertainty invading our lives.

For a long time, Phil was unable to read Andrew's bedtime story to him. Later, when he could read without crying, he resumed the ritual. Often, however, I had to leave the room. I couldn't bear the thought that Andrew might not even remember his daddy, if the cancer prevailed. So many beautiful moments with our little boy were bittersweet to us.

Phil had to undergo numerous chemotherapy regimens, as well as two back surgeries and endless hospitalizations. None of the chemotherapy made much progress against the cancer, and it was more than six months before his back was healed completely. He nearly died of infection (a major problem for myeloma patients) twice during the first year after diagnosis, and was hospitalized 14 times in the first 12-month period.

Throughout this time, we struggled to find some good in each day. We didn't want to let cancer take over our lives, so we celebrated silver linings wherever we could find them. One of these was my custom of giving Phil a single flower in celebration of completing each round of chemotherapy. As time wore on, he received many flowers. Roses, daisies, daffodils, chrysanthemums . . . beautiful blossoms marking painful milestones.

The flowers were not able to shield us from the fact that the chemotherapy that took so much from Phil was not beating the cancer. Finally, the oncologist ordered an extremely aggressive type of chemo in hopes of getting better results. Knowing that this regimen was going to have even tougher side effects, I decided Phil's homecoming flower this time had to be very special. Since it was December, I went to a garden center nearby and selected a live black spruce tree that was about 2-1/2 feet tall. I decorated it and set it on the hearth of our fireplace, where Phil would see it when I brought him home.

Phil liked the tree very much, and so did Andrew. Even though he didn't completely understand, I told Andrew that the tree was very special. I said it was Daddy's tree and that we would plant it in the back yard after Christmas. And so we did. My three older children, all young adults, helped us plant it. Under Kerry's watchful eye, Jay and Mike dragged the tree to the back yard, where it suddenly looked much smaller than it had by the fireplace.

I told Andrew we would see how fast both he and Daddy's tree grew. As usual for us, it was a bittersweet occasion. As I snapped a picture of Phil and Andrew by the tree that cold winter day, I wondered if the tree would survive the winter. And I wondered if Phil would stand next to it again with Andrew next Christmastime.

The years have flown past and today the tree has grown to a majestic 12 feet tall. Andrew is now eleven years old and still likes to have his picture taken with Daddy's Tree. As I prepare to snap the shot, Phil takes his place next to Andrew. The photo records the child, the tree and the man, all still growing. My heart records a miracle, a celebration, a gift of God. A "flower" surviving the hard, cold winter of despair, spared against all odds to bloom anew.

Angels of the Universe

We look far afield sometimes for heroes and heroines in our world, but there's no need. Many are right here in front of us. For example, I consider nurses to be true, heaven-sent angels of the universe. They staff your child's school clinic. They patch you up in the emergency room. They shuttle back and forth through the cubicles at your doctor's office. They staff nursing homes, visiting nurse services and hospice facilities. They risk their lives (and sometimes lose their lives, though we barely acknowledge it) in mobile medical units in war zones. They bring life into the world when babies are born, and ease those who are leaving life behind.

Nurses are the ones who, after the doctor leaves the room, tell you the practical details about the procedure you're about to have. They are the ones who know what to do if a caregiver has trouble learning to give injections, clean surgical sites or treat bedsores. At the hospital, they are the ones who phone the physician when the pain meds are not working, or when the patient takes a turn for the worse. They are the ones weeding through reams of paperwork in patients' files. They are the ones deciphering physicians' orders. They are the ones running through the hospital corridors, sometimes without time to catch their breath, let alone a meal. They are the people who hold you when you cry and even, sometimes (though you probably don't realize it), cry on your behalf.

Nurses are caring, compassionate, professional people who give of themselves unsparingly all day long (followed, sometimes, by all *night* long). Though they've come a long way in obtaining the professional recognition they so richly deserve, their working conditions are still difficult; their contributions too often still unnoticed.

Nurses of the world, I'm here to tell you: *I have noticed. And I thank you, from the bottom of my heart.*

I noticed the surgical nurses who took great care of my husband, following his various cancer-related surgeries. I noticed the highly skilled oncology nurses who treated him during his numerous hospitalizations, taking the time to make sure he was comfortable, helping to entice him to eat and even casting the occasional professional eye on me. I will never forget the male nurse who sometimes sat with Phil in the dark, despairing nights, sharing some of his own private pain to help alleviate Phil's. Currently, I notice the oncology nurses who still minister to Phil each month at the cancer center.

I saw the feisty nurse (thanks, Molly) who ran interference to keep an over-zealous resident out of Phil's room, when the visit and the proposed procedure were both unwarranted. I experienced a moment of soft, golden comfort amidst the black fog of despair when my baby was welcomed to the oncology floor by a nurse (thanks again, Molly dear), who said, with the voice of an angel, "Oh, we *love* babies up here!"

I noticed when another compassionate nurse, Regina, took pains to treat the entire patient, not just the disease, by praying for us and offering Phil a rosary. And then there was Amy, a quiet angel who helped me learn how to be an effective advocate for my husband and who gave Phil excellent care. I noticed Madge, an administrative professional who never forgot for one minute that she was a nurse at the bedside long before she was pushing papers. And there was Fran, a superb visiting nurse, who gave Phil devoted attention and peace of mind at home (and me the confidence to learn how to give shots).

I notice my friends, Marilyn and Kitty, who are always ready to answer my (often bizarre) medical questions. I notice my future daughter-in-law, Lois, a dedicated pediatric nurse who makes the unthinkable bearable for her little patients and their families. She also gave gentle, expert nursing assistance to my brother, Brian, following his cancer surgery; in fact, she began ministering to him just seconds after she met him, though she entered the room as a visitor, not his nurse.

Like our mother before him, my brother himself is a nurse—a nurse who has worked in emergency rooms, a state prison, mental health facilities and at a school for the deaf. He has worked with AIDS patients, and in a bariatric surgery clinic. Brian has helped countless people with his nursing skills, even when not on duty. His was the presence that comforted me most when Phil was first diagnosed with cancer, because I could relax a bit, just knowing Brian was there.

And then there's Rani. When she first brought healing into my life she wasn't yet a nurse; she was my employee, and soon became a dear friend. She saw beyond my "public" face, right into my heart, and helped me confront some hidden hurts. She fiercely championed my need to rest, and urged me to follow my inner yearnings. Later on, I was happy to return the favor, encouraging her to hear her own calling, to give nursing a try. After all, she had already mastered the most important part of the job description: she cared.

I must interject a few non-nurse angels here, starting with my husband's oncologist, Dr. Sandra Hazra. The woman is absolutely, positively an angel—a warrior angel girded for battle, filled with determination, skill and courage. In addition to nurses, I will never forget the dedicated and oh-so-kind nursing assistants, cleaning ladies, secretaries and volunteers who made our endless hospital visits almost (almost!) like coming home.

Thanks, nurses (and other medical professionals) everywhere, for all that you do to enhance and save lives. You are, truly, the angels of the universe.

Renaissance

The man walked slowly along the beach, head down, a baseball cap shielding his bearded face, his steps deliberate. He was pale and thin; at first glance, he appeared to be old, tired, ailing. The wind whipping against his shirt flattened it, revealing the outline of a necklace or similar bumpy object, hidden beneath.

As the day grew warmer, the man began to respond, like a flower turning its face toward the sun. He moved more confidently. He stopped to examine shells in the sand, ventured a few steps into the ocean, and smiled at a sandpiper, scurrying along the water's edge.

Feeling the sun's warmth, the man hesitated. Then, as if after some internal struggle, he shyly removed his shirt, revealing surgical tubing that disappeared within his chest. A scar several inches long was visible on his side, below the ribs. Another, longer one could be seen on his back. It was clear now that this man was not old, but middle aged, and that he had suffered much, and endured much. It was also clear that he was being reborn, right before my eyes, through the joint efforts of the ocean, the sunshine, and the mercy of God.

A Child Shall Lead Them

Children's concerts always make me cry. This has nothing to do with whether or not they sing off-key; it doesn't matter whether I know the children, or what songs they perform. For me, tears just flow when I hear children sing.

I experienced this emotional response again recently, at my son's holiday concert. The school's third, fourth and fifth grade students gathered at the high school to perform for their assembled families and friends. Why did the concert take place at the high school? Because our children receive so much support for their concerts that the grade school isn't big enough to hold everyone.

Seeing all those loving parents, grandparents, siblings and friends eagerly watching the children—enjoying them all but eyes riveted on their own particular little star—is the first thing that triggers the tears. As I furtively dab at my eyes with a tissue, I think of how much a caring family means to the future success of a child. And I think of the many children in the world who don't have concerts, or may not have parents who care enough to watch them sing, or may not have parents at all. And I ache for them and wonder how they will grow up properly without such support.

As each group takes the stage, I am struck first by how different each child is, one from the other. There is an amazing range in height, weight, attitude and clothing choices. For instance, some of the girls are dressed in long gowns, as if they just stepped out of a wedding procession, while others are attired in casual pants and shirts that don't quite match, looking as though they just ran in from the playground. The same is true of the boys' sartorial choices: a few wear ties; a couple even wear suits, while others wear sweats and athletic shoes—and most wear something in between.

The children's faces and body language are irresistible to me. A few of the kids keep their eyes trained on the music teacher, as if their very lives depend on paying attention. Some, especially the boys, struggle with the effort to stand still and not fidget. Others can be seen moving in time to the beat, while a few in each group (usually girls) act as taskmasters, casting a critical eye on their neighbors, ready to nudge those who fail to perform properly. Others, stage struck, are overly conscious of their own small selves; they play to the audience, striking poses, mouthing the words, and noticing the effect on the audience. Hollywood, here they come!

I first smile and then laugh delightedly at the children's antics. Their innocence, their thinly veiled motives are so natural, so real. They haven't learned yet to conceal their feelings. They haven't developed the ability to hide their hearts with a mask of politeness, to cloak their true selves somewhere deep inside. They are new, fresh-faced . . . absolutely gorgeous.

To me, the children's performance is a microcosm of life itself. Our adult struggles to get along, to work together, to be kind to one another, are mirrored in the kids' struggles to sing in unison, to be forbearing towards a classmate who keeps forgetting the words, and to stay on key.

As I snap a picture of them, I wish so much that the camera could freeze them at this moment in time, so they could stay forever as they are right now. I wish that they could stay here, where they are loved and secure. I don't know their personal stories; I'm sure some of the kids are already dealing with painful struggles we can't see, but at least for this one moment, they are being cherished. Someone cared enough to bring them here. Someone cared enough to watch them perform.

When I look at their innocent faces, I see the entire world. Every race, every socio-economic level is represented here; many religious beliefs and values, many countries of origin, too, are embodied by these precious children. The songs they sing come from every land too—songs that celebrate the common threads among us, no matter what beliefs have shaped us.

I see in the children hope for the future. So often, as adults, we focus on our differences rather than our similarities. We become almost paralyzed by political correctness. We aren't sure what to say to a Jewish friend about Hanukkah, or to a Muslim neighbor about Ramadan, or to an African-American friend who may celebrate Kwanzaa. Christians celebrate Christmas, but so do many others who aren't religious at all. In our concern about saying the wrong thing, we say nothing, thus losing an opportunity to learn.

The children know better. They are curious and ask each other, often bluntly, about their differing traditions. They celebrate together, just as they sing together. They take for granted that love and peace and forbearance are desired by everyone, at the holidays (no matter whose holidays they may be) and always.

The children sing of love, peace and the birth of love in their hearts. Can you hear them? The children, God love them, are leading us. Will you follow?

Could It Be Magic?

It happens when you least expect it. You can't make it happen at will; it enters your life on its own terms, always quite suddenly; almost like magic. How lucky we are to be surrounded, each and every day, by those electrifying flashes of "something more," those exotic moments that amaze us, and grace our lives with unexpected joy.

Have you ever been walking in the woods and suddenly heard the melodious tinkle of a nearby stream? A magical water song, so subtle, so quiet that it would go unnoticed in a less tranquil setting. No louder than a desktop water fountain, it is much more soulful, and so compelling.

And flowers! I've always considered flowers to be among the most exquisite creations on earth. They are like jewels, glowing in every conceivable color, shape and size. Their endless, opulent variations delight us; their diversity exceeds even our own! Think of the beauty of a single blossom—just one! And then consider that, wherever we go in the world, even in the desert, flowers are blooming, just waiting to dazzle us with their brilliance. What wealth they represent!

Recently, I was overtaken by incredible magic in, of all places, the parking lot at a Lowe's store. As we walked to our car, my husband and I were amazed to see a sunset of such splendor, such majesty, such beautiful shades of pink and mauve, that we stopped in our tracks to savor it. Sadly, most people were hurrying in and out of the store with shopping lists in hand and home fix-up projects on their minds; few even noticed the artistry decorating the evening sky overhead.

One of the most spiritual experiences of my life was evoked by a spectacular sunrise. Being a morning person, I have witnessed many sunrises, but none so moving as this one, which I saw while on vacation in Nags Head, North Carolina, several years ago. It was a pearly-pink, iridescent sun, gradually appearing around the edge of the balcony of the condo just above ours, framed perfectly by the overhang. The world was so utterly quiet, so entirely peaceful that I felt I could almost hear the magnificent orb emerging slowly, softly, from the sea. Though no photo could do it justice, I did snap a shot of it, which now resides in my Bible, to remind me that pure joy comes in many forms, and can arrive anytime, unbidden and spontaneously.

And, what could be more magical than the unexpected glimpse of deer, right in one's own back yard? Honored with such a visit occasionally, I am always spellbound. I see movement out of the corner of my eye as I pass a window . . . and there they are! I feel wealthy, blessed, to see such graceful creatures, so shy and beautiful, so mesmerizing that I literally hold my breath, so as not to scare them away.

There is a bountiful patch of fennel growing against our house. Many times I've groused about it, saying that it is untidy, too tall, not pretty. But on certain summer days, at about four o'clock in the afternoon, sunlight slants across the plants. Small bees lazily drift over the fennel, creating a stunning display, as both plants and bees are bathed in golden light.

I suppose, along with the late John Lennon, I could be called a dreamer. Perhaps not everyone can see the magic that I see in a tinkling stream. Some would fuss about pollution or mosquitoes instead. One could miss the beauty of flowers if all they saw was weeds. Perhaps one could even think that sunrises and sunsets are a dime a dozen, since they occur every single day. If you happen to be a hunter, or if you consider deer to be simply overgrown "rodents," you probably can't relate to why I think they are so magical. And if you worry about being stung, you may not see the magic in my golden fennel bees.

I hope that you allow space for your own small miracles, whatever they may be . . . those mystical moments that bring magic to your life, that touch you so deeply that they stop you in your tracks, just by being there. Could it be magic? Only if you believe . . . and see.

Helping Hands

Helping hands. Often we use that term metaphorically, as a way to illustrate the love and encouragement that others offer us. Lately, though, I've been considering helping hands more literally. I've been noticing the mystical language of hands—the hope, comfort and support they offer those in need.

For example, consider the recent story in the news about a baby girl who had been kidnapped from her mother's van. As I watched a live broadcast of the family reunion on television, I couldn't stop noticing the hands. First, I noticed the young mother's hands, heavily bandaged—evidence of the valiant struggle she had endured to protect her child. Next, at the edge of the TV screen, I notice a man's hand, perhaps that of a relative or a police officer, cupping the young mother's elbow, as if to protect her or to guide her steps.

The baby's father stood close to his wife, his hand hovering near her while, in the background, someone else's hand supported him. The television shot showed the mother's hands, reaching out to her baby in utter joy. And, a moment later, an older woman, undoubtedly a grandmother, extended her hands, trembling with emotion, to touch the little one. I suspect there was another moment, not captured by cameras, when, throughout America, the hands of those watching grabbed a tissue, to dry tears of happiness for a family mercifully reunited.

We see the manacled hands of a militant, alleged to have masterminded the killing of many, clasped defiantly above his head. We see the hands of Palestinian and Israeli mothers, covering their faces as they cry in grief. We see dozens of hands around the world, carrying loved ones to final resting places, while other hands lovingly prepare meals to comfort the living. We see attorneys, often with tears in their eyes, putting a supportive arm around their clients as the sentence is received. We see the hands of young soldiers, tenderly shepherding a mother and child to a place of safety.

Not long ago, we saw numerous hands, working frantically, operating pumps, holding each other's hands in hope, wiping away tears of anguish, raising hands heavenward in prayer, and then finally, finally, lifting nine trapped miners—alive—out of what we had feared would be their tomb.

In a small town, we see unselfish, generous hands, pitching in to clean up the devastation caused by a tornado. We see hands folded in prayer, hands putting offerings in collection baskets. We see football fans, young and old, leaning down from the stands, straining to get a player's autograph during training camp. We see those same fans, pumping their fists triumphantly in the air, at numerous victory celebrations. We see hands "high fiving," applauding, creating works of art, scrubbing floors. We see plump, tiny toddlers' hands, held aloft, learning to wave "bye-bye."

We see Bruce Springsteen's hands on his guitar, fingering it with such intimacy that the instrument seems like an extension of his body, his heart. We see the hand of a police officer as he embraces his wife, his face hidden in the comfort of her neck, wordlessly seeking sustenance, answers, as he attends the wake of his brother officer, shot down for no reason. We see the hand of the slain officer's widow, with a world of unshed tears waiting in her eyes, protectively encircling her baby daughter. We see that baby's tiny hand, resting in utter trust and innocence on her mother's arm. We see a multitude of hands, of every race, every walk of life, joined together in fervent prayers for peace in our world.

Recently, driving on the expressway, I saw the aftermath of a multi-car accident. Several men, with strong yet gentle hands, had pulled a young woman out of an overturned vehicle and were placing her, with utmost care, on the grass. Other hands were outstretched, offering bottles of water to those in need, while still others clasped cell phones, calling for help . . . help that would be delivered by the caring, professional hands of paramedics and police officers, nurses and doctors.

I see my mother-in-law's hands, knotted and gnarled with arthritis, endlessly baking and cooking for her family. Her hands tremble now, yet she cups each of our faces, tenderly, as she kisses us goodbye. Her long life's journey has been enhanced, for over 65 years, by the presence of her husband, whose strikingly large, capable hands once toiled endlessly, in hard physical labor . . . and yet have softly nurtured a stream of children, grandchildren and great-grandchildren, with utmost care.

Whether elegant or callused, small or large, the hands of others uplift us, support us and, indeed, serve as the hands of the Creator on earth. The hands of family, friends, co-workers and even strangers arrive, often mysteriously or unexpectedly, whenever we need them. They are freely given to us, these hands filled with care and concern, ready to share our joy or pain, to hold us up or pull us back. They are the personification of all that is best in the human spirit. They are symbols of love, and messengers of hope. Aren't hands magnificent?

An Attitude of Gratitude

In the springtime, people call the air conditioner repair shop to schedule routine service. "Can you send someone out to check my A/C? See if anything needs to be adjusted?" Some of us may realize, much to our dismay, that the 1040 we recently mailed to Uncle Sam wasn't quite right, so we have to file an amendment to adjust it. We are sure that we have found Ms. or Mr. Right, only to recognize that we were wrong. So we are forced to adjust to the fact that the search for our soul mate must continue. Where I live, in Ohio, we often are lucky enough to find ourselves having to adjust to unseasonably warm weather—just a day or two after an unseasonable snowfall. So we put down the snow shovel and whip out our shorts and sandals. Life is full of adjustments.

I don't know about you, but I find that one of the things in life that most often needs adjustment is my own attitude about things. Though I try to maintain a positive outlook, I find, all too often, that I've slipped into the pit of negativity. So I have to drag my weary carcass—now covered in mud and weeds—out of the hole and back into the sunshine.

We all need an attitude tune-up occasionally. So often, we slip into focusing on what is *wrong* in our lives, instead of on what's *right*. It's too bad, because we miss so much that way. How can we avoid the negativity trap? How can we get out of Adversity Plaza and move to a new address on the sunny side of the street? Develop a Gratitude Attitude. Here is just one example that illustrates my point.

My beloved mother died on November 4, 1986, which happened to be Election Day. Mom strongly believed voting was both a responsibility and an honor, so nothing ever kept her from the polls. Actually, nothing ever kept her from nagging us kids about voting, either—even years before we were old enough to do so. If you happen to have been blessed (cursed?) with an Italian mother of your own, I'm sure you can easily visualize the entire scenario, which of course included, along with the nagging, fervent glances heavenward, as she implored God to help her make us into upstanding, voting citizens.

Therefore, it seemed ironic that Mom would die, rather suddenly, on Election Day, without getting a chance to vote. A few days after the funeral, however, we found a postcard in Mom's mailbox from the Board of Elections, thanking her for her absentee ballot. She *had* voted one last time, after all! We were amazed but, knowing Mom, perhaps we shouldn't have been. All I know is, I laughed with relief, awash in gratitude. It lightened my grief, you see, to know that Mom wasn't denied that last opportunity to vote. It was comforting to know that, just like the posthumous postcard from the Board of Elections, the gifts Mom had given me throughout my life would continue to flow. And so I was thankful.

Sometimes we think we can't feel gratitude until we reach some arbitrary goal. We can't stop to notice everyday triumphs. We have to strive for the BIG success—the raise, the wedding, landing that big client, etc. We can't feel gratitude when life is handing us lemons . . . or can we? Why not make them into lemonade?

We often cannot control the events in our lives. But we can control our response to what happens. If we can live in the moment, find the good even in bad situations, smell the flowers, examine a snowflake, kiss a child, or experience the love in another's eyes, we truly have it all. With a gratitude attitude, we recognize that we are surrounded by abundance . . . not just on landmark occasions, but always. Isn't that superb? Isn't it wonderful? Isn't it worth celebrating, every day? Please, do it now.

Sixth Stop:

The Wall of Mirrors

This time, as we look in the dusty windows, we see . . . ourselves! The room inside, once a dance studio, is bare of almost everything except a wall of mirrors that invites us to see our true reflection. Will you take the risk of feeling a bit awkward? Will you accept the invitation to grow, to change, to join the dance? Are you ready to see yourself clearly, as you glide back and forth in front of the Wall of Mirrors?

*   *   *

What Makes Your Heart Sing?

The photo reveals a young girl, perhaps 10 or 11 years old, tall and skinny, as awkward as a young colt, offering the camera a shy grin. And like a colt, she liked to run around and around in the emerald green summer grass, experiencing pure joy in the delicious sense of freedom, the wind whipping through her long black hair, a smile on her face, her cares left far behind.

Even the chill of winter didn't dampen the girl's enthusiasm for running, though this was long ago, when the snow really *was* deeper, when winter was an entire season of white, when a single snowfall blanketed the earth for weeks at a time. Even then, the girl ran around and around the field, blazing a trail through the white wilderness, marking out a small world of her own, where she could be herself. She even built hurdles, and added wild leaps to her mad dashes around the field.

When she wasn't running, she was reading, writing and listening to music. She didn't question what she was drawn to, what moved her. She was one with life, filled with life. She felt energized, triumphant and capable of awe-inspiring achievements.

The skinny girl with the boundless energy and wild mane of black hair was left behind, long ago, as I learned the lessons of the "real" world—one of which, at that time, was that sports were only for boys. Eventually, with no role models to emulate, I lost interest in running and other athletics. In fact, later I often described myself as "uncoordinated" and "not athletic at all."

Recently, however, as middle age has settled more or less gracefully upon me (not that *I* have graciously settled into *IT*), I've begun to examine my life a bit. One of my goals has been to recall what I was like as a child, before the "shoulds," the "no's" and the "you can't do that's" kicked in. What interests had been dearest to my heart? Could I, in hindsight, look back and see the early budding of any particular talents or dreams?

So far, I've discovered three significant facts: Though it took decades for me to acknowledge and begin developing my talent, I know now that I'm a writer, and have been since an early age. I passionately love music, of many different kinds. And though it makes me laugh to imagine myself as a jock, I now suspect I have some innate, undeveloped athletic ability lurking within. Wow! It's like someone just told me that I actually have blue eyes, despite ample evidence to the contrary!

Let's look at another, more recent snapshot. We see a middle-aged woman, still with dark hair (albeit now threaded with silver), no longer exactly skinny, wearing an oversized tee shirt, shorts, and running shoes. She is grinning triumphantly from ear to ear. Has she won a marathon? Qualified for the Olympics? Not quite. She has simply completed her daily 30-minute walk/run through her neighborhood. This time, she ran more than half the distance. And she was thrilled.

What's the importance of this? How does it relate to you? I think it's so easy for us to get sidetracked as we go through life— sidetracked from pursuits that we really enjoy, things for which we have true talent. We squeeze ourselves into square holes, though we are round pegs. We choose our college or our career or our marriage partner according to family expectations, how "safe" the choice feels, or who else lives in the neighborhood. We remember other kids taunting us about how stupid we are, how lacking in grace or competitiveness we are, and we take it to heart so much that we regretfully, or even unknowingly, let go of what matters, what makes us whole, what makes our heart sing.

Let your mind drift back to an earlier time, when you were quite young. What did you like to do then? How did it make you feel? What has happened to your participation or enjoyment of it in the years since then? Is there something that made you feel so alive, so happy, that you smile even now, just remembering it?

If so, I urge you to have the courage to face the awkwardness you might feel, the "I'm too old," or the "I can't do that anymore." The essence of that youngster is still within, calling you to be carefree, to play again. Reclaim that confident, adventurous being who is the *real* you. If you can't reclaim it all, go for what you *can* achieve.

That's exactly what I'm doing. Though I'll never be a great runner, I dash along, rather slowly, a bit awkwardly, but finally running *my* race, as only I can run it. For just a moment each day, as I turn my face to the wind, I am that little girl again, young and carefree. Listening to Pavarotti on my earphones, I inwardly match him, note for soaring, thrilling note. Columns, articles, books and poems spring to fruition in my mind as I run along. In these moments, I am free, I am truly the "me" I was meant to be! So, please, if I falter along the way, if my tired legs or overtaxed lungs give way, don't be concerned. Just press "rewind" on my Walkman, adjust my earphones and leave me there. I assure you I'll be fine because, having reclaimed my real, inner self, my precious talents and interests, I'm already in a far, far better place. I am home!

Nothing to Fear
But Fear Itself

She looks nervously over her shoulder as she walks down the street. She drives carefully, defensively, obsessed with keeping out of harm's way, knowing that she must stay safe if she is to protect her family in the dark days ahead. She gazes at her sleeping children in the middle of the night, praying for their safety in a suddenly uncertain world. She is on high alert day and night, because she no longer feels secure. The enemy has invaded her life on all sides. Has the world gone mad? Where the hell is God in all this?

Her heart pounds wildly every time she picks up the telephone, bracing herself for bad news. She avoids watching television, except late at night. Then, she cries while watching M.A.S.H. reruns. Her tired mind goes in circles, trying to imagine how she can protect her children from what is to come, how she can keep their world safe, at least for a little longer. Their innocence, she fears, is already gone. She is grief-stricken, angry that she cannot shield them from the harshness of life. Isn't that her job as a mother?

Her husband is unable to comfort her because he now lives in a different world, apart from his family. He valiantly tries to fight the good fight against a formidable foe. He straps on his battle gear each day, staggers to his feet, and tries to defend himself, for his family's sake. He is cloaked in despair sometimes, not knowing how the battle will end, but fearing that he won't survive. So much has already been lost, taken from him in an instant—his livelihood, his daily routines, his freedom, his dignity, his sense of security. All the rules have changed. His life has become a nightmare. He is swathed in devastation, his life in ruins.

Does some part of the above scenario ring true to you? Have you been experiencing similar feelings of loneliness, fear and hopelessness lately? Do you feel that your life is being defined by circumstances, instead of by you? If so, welcome to my world. No, I'm not talking about the world we've lived in, all of us here in America, since September 11, 2001. I'm referring, instead, to the world my family has lived in since January 25, 1993, the day my husband was diagnosed with multiple myeloma, an incurable form of cancer. I'm referring to the loss of innocence, the loss of routine, the loss of security that my own family, and countless other families, face each day.

We are people who, long before September 11, had already been visited by painful events, by tragedies beyond our control. We were already marked by invisible scars, caused by cancer, Alzheimer's, multiple sclerosis, homelessness, poverty, mental and physical handicaps, the loss of a spouse or a child, and every other illness, setback, or grief you can imagine. We, like you, were innocents one day, broken-hearted the next. And our lives were forever changed. But don't despair, please. My goal, as you enter my world, is to comfort you, to point out the markers of hope and joy, and to help you find your way back to peace.

A well-meaning woman once said to me, "How can you get up every morning, knowing that your husband is going to die?" I replied, as gently as possible, "How do YOU get up every day, knowing that YOUR husband is going to die?" She was a bit startled, so I explained that we are all going to die eventually, but none of us actually knows when.

We comfort ourselves with illusions, until something forces us to see that we're not really in control, that life offers no promises. If anything, those of us who have lost the illusion of "forever" are ahead of the game. Our lives have taken on a new richness, a depth of color and contentment that wasn't there before. We eventually learned how to live in the moment, because it is a profound truth that yesterday is gone, and tomorrow is a question mark. Today is all we have. And it's all *you* have. Live for today, don't worry about tomorrow, which is beyond your control, and you will experience greater joy than ever before.

Seeing oneself as a victim—whatever the circumstances—is a choice. Right after my husband's diagnosis, I believed no one had it as bad as we did. After all, we had a 7-month old son who might lose his father. I had three older children who loved my husband (their stepfather) dearly and didn't deserve to lose him. It just didn't seem fair at all. But soon, seeing with new eyes, hearing with new ears, living in this new world that I had not wanted to enter, I saw others who were struggling with situations worse than my own. I saw people who refused to relinquish their inner power. They still laughed, though sometimes through tears. They somehow emerged victorious. Even in the face of painful uncertainties, they showed me how to stand up, be thankful for blessings, give of myself to others, and keep on trucking.

Whenever one has losses, it seems, one also somehow receives blessings. My husband would never have asked for cancer, but the grace, the blessings that have come from it are easy to discover. We learn, in time, that life ebbs and flows. Painful events will occur, but so will joyous celebrations.

So what's the answer? How do we deal with uncertain times? The best antidote to fear and pain, to uncertainty and misery, is to remain in control of our responses. We have no choice in life about much that happens to us, but we do have a choice about whether or not we will live in fear. So let's not focus on worst case scenarios, especially since most of them will never happen. Let's focus instead on loving our families, our country, our friends, our enemies and everyone else. As Franklin D. Roosevelt once said, "We have nothing to fear but fear itself."

The Carrot Philosophy

"Eat your carrots." It was my mother's mantra, and probably your mom's too. It's what I said to my three older kids many years ago, and it's what I say these days to my youngest child.

Recently, as I was washing some "baby" carrots to put in Andrew's lunchbox, I gave some thought to the life of a carrot, that valuable veggie that kids will actually eat. "Baby carrots" is quite a concept, isn't it? I always visualize some adorable toddler carrot, being ripped away from its mother prematurely, just to make humans' lunch packing easier. I was quite relieved when I learned recently that baby carrots are actually full-size veggies, machine cut to their cute baby size, then cleaned and bagged.

I'm sure by now you're wondering if I'm actually going to devote this entire story to carrots. I'm not, but perhaps I should.

You see, I'm trying to learn how to live "mindfully," which means, among other things, allowing time to smell the roses, savor the moment . . . and consider the carrots. It's not easy for me. I'm a hyper, mind-always-working type of person. I have brushed aside far more important matters than carrots in my rush to get more done, more quickly. Sometimes I'm so harried that I feel I'll hyperventilate if I stop for even one second.

But I'm intrigued by the concept of mindfulness. Its meaning is simple: live in the moment, whether you're washing carrots, sitting in traffic or folding laundry. Be aware of the colors and textures—

the bright orange of the carrots, the sunshine slanting across the traffic-clogged road. Think about the family member whose laundry you're folding as you fold it.

I'm here to tell you, this is not easy, and I can't do it for sustained periods of time so far, but it is rewarding. It reminds me that "frantic" is a choice. It reminds me that paying attention to what I'm doing may even result in its being finished sooner or better. And it illustrates that the task of carrot washing *is* my life, at least for that moment. In the rush to get to the next task, we miss out on our very lives, because real life is contained in the car wash moment, the standing in line moment . . . the carrot moment.

I do not sew, other than mending minor rips and replacing buttons. When I get out a needle and thread, it becomes almost a ceremony ("Mom's going to sew on my button!"). I avoid it as long as possible but, once I start, I get absorbed in what I'm doing. As I poke the needle through the button, I think of my son, and how fast he's growing up, and how big the shirt was when he first began wearing it. I sew my hopes and dreams for him right onto that shirt, along with the button.

I rarely make my mother's special chicken-fried steak anymore. For one thing, the "old kids" aren't here that often and it's too much work to make it for only Phil, Andrew and me. It's pretty high in fat, too.

But when I do make it, as I dip each piece of meat in an egg and milk mixture, then dredge it in the flour, breadcrumbs and seasonings, I think of Mom. I remember her wonderful meals, and much more. I recall how, as a young bride, I just couldn't get my chicken-fried steak to turn out like hers, but now I can. My kids will always remember it as *their* mother's chicken-fried steak, just as I think of it as my mother's. It has become a family legacy.

Being mindful of the moment extends far beyond domestic tasks. It can improve our relationships with everyone we hold dear. How often, it seems, we half-listen to others. How often we try to do several things at once, sure that we can give adequate attention to each. How often, I wonder, are we wrong about that? How often do our loved ones feel brushed aside, unimportant, when just a few seconds of eye contact, a brief moment of our full attention, would assure them we're listening?

So, no matter how busy you are, why not pause for just a few seconds as you do each task? As you're raking leaves, consider the journey the leaves have taken from green to red or yellow, from tree to ground. It'll be less of a chore and you'll feel more alive. How about getting out a magnifying glass to examine a single snowflake? It will take you into a new world, one in which each snowflake is a work of art, rather than a pain in the patootie.

Enjoy the moment. After all, it's the only one you have.

Life Lessons from the Velveteen Rabbit

Do you remember the classic book, *The Velveteen Rabbit*, by Margery Williams? It's the delightful story of a stuffed bunny that becomes real. And, like most great children's books, this one offers a meaningful message for people of all ages. In essence, we learn from the Rabbit's journey that love can make us "real." We find that becoming real is often an uncomfortable process—but well worth it just the same.

The Velveteen Rabbit belonged to a little boy who carried him everywhere he went. Gradually, his handling of the Rabbit caused its velveteen fur to wear away. His kisses caused the pink to wear off of the bunny's nose. His hugs left the Rabbit's seams loose and his innards saggy. But in the final analysis, the Bunny became real . . . and his losses became unimportant.

Isn't that how it is with us, too? The very experiences that cause us the most pain often become the pathway to tremendous growth. Let's listen to a conversation between the Velveteen Rabbit and his friend, the Skin Horse, which marks the beginning of the Rabbit's journey towards becoming real.

"What is REAL?" asked the Rabbit one day, when he and the Skin Horse were lying side by side in the nursery. "Does it mean having things that buzz inside you and a stick-out handle?"

"Real isn't how you are made," said the Skin Horse. "It's a thing that happens to you."

"Does it hurt?" asked the Rabbit.

"Sometimes," said the Skin Horse, for he was always truthful. "When you are real, though, you don't mind being hurt."

"Does it happen all at once, like being wound up," the Rabbit asked, "or bit by bit?"

"It doesn't happen all at once," said the Skin Horse. "You *become*. It takes a long time."

The boy continued to love the Velveteen Rabbit, taking his beloved companion wherever he went. In the process, the Rabbit became more and more unsightly—at least to the rest of the world. But the Rabbit was so happy that he never even noticed how shabby he was becoming. That's because his focus was on loving the boy and on becoming real.

And the Rabbit's dedication was rewarded. One day, the boy's nanny was annoyed when he insisted on having the Velveteen Rabbit at bedtime. She said: "It's just a toy." But the boy said: "You mustn't say that. He isn't a toy. He's REAL!"

When the little Rabbit heard this he was very happy. He knew he was no longer merely a stuffed bunny. The boy himself had said it: he was *real!* The Rabbit was so happy he could scarcely contain himself. As the story tells us, "he was almost too happy to sleep, and so much love stirred in his little sawdust heart that it almost burst. Into his boot-button eyes came a look of wisdom and beauty, so that even Nana noticed it the next morning . . ."

However, even when we know we are real, the road can be difficult, as the Velveteen Rabbit found out. The boy became quite ill and, when he recovered, his bunny was discarded. (The doctor, you see, thought he was full of germs.) While lying on a pile of trash, the Rabbit felt that being real didn't help him much. Despair overtook him. He said to himself: "Of what use is it to be loved and become real if it all ends like this?"

Don't we question this ourselves? Even if we've done the work needed to become real, even if we're doing our very best, don't we lose our way sometimes? In the end, though, the Velveteen Rabbit triumphed . . . and we can too!

Margery Williams' beautiful tale goes on to tell us that, as the bunny lay crying on the trash heap, he was visited by a beautiful fairy. She gathered him up in her arms and kissed him on his velveteen nose. "I am the nursery magic fairy," she said. "I take care of all the playthings that the children have loved. When they are old and worn out and the children don't need them any more, then I come and take them away with me and turn them into Real."

"Wasn't I real before?" asked the little Rabbit.

"You were real to the boy," the fairy said, "because he loved you. Now you shall be real to everyone."

So the fairy made him into a Real Rabbit. He gave a leap of joy and began whirling around and around with the other rabbits in the woods nearby. His reward had come at last. He was real!

Take comfort in the Rabbit's beautiful story when you find it difficult to be real. Life *is* hard sometimes . . . but it's also filled with joy.

Simplicity

Simplicity. We yearn for it, perhaps because we've created a way of life that is anything but simple. We are surrounded by technological wonders that were supposed to make our lives easier—cell phones, email, computers, pagers—but which instead have stolen much of our peacefulness.

How to regain simplicity? We can make conscious decisions to be surrounded by fewer objects. We can choose *not* to continuously upgrade to the newest and biggest (houses, furnishings, cars, technology). We can choose to schedule less; rest more. However, change is hard to implement so, for many of us, vacation time is the only time we commit ourselves to slowing down, savoring the ordinary, and simply "be-ing."

Of course, the secret is to take the "right" kind of vacation—a relaxing, slow-paced one. A vacation at the beach, for example, puts us in touch with simple pleasures. After a day or two of "decompressing" from our frantic everyday life, time seems to slow down. Our bodies relax; languishing in repose is the only thing on the agenda. Delightful subtleties become celebrations. Is the sea a bit greener today? Can you see the faint pinkish tinge in this white shell?

Complexities are left behind. We pack lightly. We focus on the essentials in life—food, shelter, nature and each other. We become content to simply sit or walk near the water's edge. We intently examine tiny treasures from the sea. We take notice of subtle changes in the waves. We watch, fascinated, as pelicans swoop down into the ocean to catch fish.

The ocean is ideally suited to simple living. The wind sweeps our cares and concerns away; the constant movement of the waves seems to smooth our rough edges, just as it smoothes the rocks and shells along the shore. Boats navigating the waves beckon us to see life's "big picture"—the vast world just beyond the horizon. The power of a storm sweeping in makes us realize how tiny and vulnerable we really are.

As we give way to simplicity, we may pay less attention to our appearance. We don't worry about the wrinkles (in our faces or in our clothes). We leave makeup, toupees, and dignity behind as we revel in the simple life of the sea. We are anonymous here, anyway. The sea reminds us that, in the most profoundly human sense, we are all the same. Since everyone is dressed in shorts or swimsuits, status is left behind. Without seeing their everyday attire, where they live or what kind of car they drive, we have no idea if a fellow vacationer is a bank president, a cleaning lady, a minister or a famous author. Strangers smile kindly at one another as they walk along the shore. Everyone is relaxed, serene, immersed in simply being fully alive.

Simplicity makes us more primitive, more real. We become explorers and gatherers, fully engaged in excavating the next unique shell, building a sandcastle, or choosing what kind of seafood to have for dinner.

It is very healthy to respect something that is bigger than our selves. Our society is fixated on competition, keeping score, winning. But the sea, so powerful, reminds us that our strength and abilities are limited. This allows us to realize that there are rewards inherent in *not* being the biggest and the best. We can put down the armor, stop struggling . . . and just *be*. How comforting, how truly marvelous!

To me, simplicity, especially on the seashore, is the very definition of paradise. Just think of it: we can regain the playful, childlike joy that still lurks somewhere inside us. We laugh, carefree and focused only on the simplest of pleasures—wind, sun, and sea. We shrug off the structure and worries of everyday life. We are intoxicated with the wonder, the joy, of simply *being*.

This is the life we were meant to live—uncomplicated and free. We were created to continually expand our spirits, thereby making room for even more contentment. So, make a pact with yourself that you will let your soul come out to play, every day.

Traveling Light

Every year or so, wild fires raging out of control in the western states make the news. Articles and news reports show us weary firefighters who, with smoke-stained faces and gritty determination, struggle to hold the line against Mother Nature. We also see the anxious faces of those whose homes lie in the path of destruction—people who have had to pack up whatever belongings they could carry, leaving their beloved homes (and much of the contents) behind.

Many times, there is advance warning that fires, floods, hurricanes or other disasters are approaching. Rather than fleeing for their lives in the face of immediate danger, people may have a bit of time to pack, prior to evacuation. They determine what to take, and what must be left behind. I've often wondered how they decide. Do they rush frantically from room to room, simply grabbing whatever they can, or do they try to assess what is most valuable, choosing what cannot be replaced at any price?

Although we hope never to be faced with such decisions, the questions seem worthy of consideration. I invite you to take a few moments to ponder these questions: what would you take with you, given just a few hours to decide? What would you make room for, if the space was very limited?

First, let's make a few assumptions. We'll assume that we've already secured the safety of our most precious assets—our family and friends. Fido, Fifi, the hamsters, goldfish and assorted "creepy crawlies" have also been removed from harm's way. Our financial and legal documents are in a lock box at the bank, and we're not worrying about furniture or other replaceable items. Our practical needs, such as food, clothing and prescription medicines, have been provided.

What's left for our consideration are the special things that define who we are, those items that we treasure above all others, the sentimental, quirky or well-worn objects that warm our hearts and brighten our days—the truly irreplaceable bits and pieces of our lives.

For me, the first thing to be packed is my late mother's Bible. It holds the essence of her philosophies on life and faith, as evidenced by the various passages she underlined, the notes and holy cards tucked among the pages.

Next, I'll run through the house, snatching up family photos. A few are framed or arranged neatly in albums; most are in a large box, waiting for the day (ha!) when I'll finally organize them. Without a single word, these pictures tell the story of my life, and those of my family and friends. All the years, with their numerous celebrations, struggles and triumphs, are eloquently recorded . . . and precious beyond belief.

Yikes! I must pack up my "scribbles"—ancient articles, stories, poems and journals, ideas and notes for future columns, books, articles and poems. And my treasured "cat card"—a greeting card my daughter Kerry gave me years ago, in which she jotted down the lyrics to a Tom Petty song, *Wildflowers*, along with a very special note of her own.

Next, I grab a small, whimsical stuffed zebra that my youngest son, Andrew, gave me, which perches on my computer. And the jewelry box my second son, Mike, made for me years ago. And the pink stone with an angel imbedded in it that my oldest son,

Jay, gave me. Then I snatch up some favorite earrings and a small, vividly painted bowl that my husband gave me. And my beautiful, sapphire blue and white ceramic angel plate, a gift from my sister, Terry. And my classic edition of Louisa May Alcott's *Little Women*, given to my by my brother, Brian.

Heading for the kitchen, I grab a few examples of my 10-year-old son's artwork, and then dash down to the basement to retrieve some of my three older children's school papers, now a bit yellow around the edges, but carefully packed away.

What else? A small "Erin Go Bragh" ("Ireland Forever") pin, from the 1940's, which belonged to my Italian mother (go figure) that I wear on St. Patty's Day. And that's all, except for my precious books, and a few CD's and tapes. But wait! Is there room for Mom's battered, old 9x13" cake pan, which I still use for my kids' birthdays? As I head out the door, I grab my silly, pot-bellied wrought iron bunny, who bravely holds a whimsical flower aloft. And that's all.

What's on your list? Where does your true wealth reside? And does anything else really matter?

The Young Black Filly

At the beginning of this book, I shared my recurring "old gray mare" daydream and promised to let you know what happened to the old girl. Recently, she simply disappeared. She's out to pasture at last, resting from her labors, with my thanks for a job well done.

Some time ago, as I was driving along a highway, a new image came to mind. I had been thinking some typical midlife thoughts, about how I want to live fully; about how I don't want to be a martyr or an old gray mare; about how I want to be the "real" me. Textbook midlife stuff. Suddenly, into my mind trotted a brand-new horse, with a brand-new attitude and a brand-new mission.

She was a young filly, full of vim and vigor. She high-stepped along, slowing now to a skittish, crab-stepping walk. Her coat was glossy black; her mane and tail long and graceful. She was clearly a woman with a purpose, and the purpose was to please her own sweet self—and no one else.

At her side walked a man, his hand gently grasping her halter. They approached a beautiful, velvet-green valley, a broad vista of natural beauty as far as the eye could see. As they reached the valley, the man stroked the beautiful filly's cheek, removing her halter and speaking softly to her. Then she was off, running for the sheer joy of it, running her own race at last, running into the sunlight, the early morning dew on her hoofs, running because she was made to run, in safety and peace . . . free at last!

What was the message brought to me by the young filly? That I cannot be "The Responsible One," the "go to" person, for those around me. I can support them in appropriate ways; I can love them and enjoy them, but I cannot take full responsibility for anything or anyone except myself. The black horse reminds me, too, that I have a responsibility to live fully, to follow my dreams, and to stretch and grow in myriad ways. The young filly also tells me that I have intrinsic value, just for living and breathing . . . and so does everyone else. And she tells me that youth is an attitude, not an age, that freedom and joy can be mine at any moment I choose, no matter what might be happening around me. And most of all, she whispers that I am meant to *thrive*, not simply *survive*.

What images does *your* heart show you, in the theater of your mind? What are your dreams (or daydreams) trying to say to you? What picture of yourself do you carry in your heart? Does the picture need adjustment? Do you want to fine-tune part of it? Listen; watch; learn. Don't delay; life is short. And you don't have to remain at Adversity Plaza forever, no matter what happens. Trust me.

Conclusion

Cinnamon City

We approach a sparkling clean, welcoming storefront. Far from empty or deserted, the entrance is decorated with beautiful flowers; immaculate white curtains flutter in the spring breeze. The irresistible aroma of cinnamon tickles your nose, beckoning you to enter. You go inside.

Unseen, a friendly voice calls out from the back room: "Come right in! Welcome! Please make yourself comfortable. Help yourself to coffee or tea; the cinnamon rolls will be ready in a moment. There's just enough time for a snack before you hail your taxi."

*　　*　　*

Do you understand now? Has our walk through the Plaza been helpful to you? The bottom line is: There is a very long list of things in life that we cannot control, including illness, accidents, death, the IRS, the weather, the stock markets, other people's attitudes or behaviors, cats, sports scores, politicians, our co-workers or bosses, being downsized . . . and the list goes on. There is a glimmer of hope, however, because we can control our response to life—our attitude—no matter what is happening around us or to us.

Will there still be dark moments in life, when hopelessness will be all we can see? Of course. But, just as dawn follows darkness, joy will return. Somehow, we can eventually make tiny choices that say "Yes!" to life. It may be as simple as getting out of bed in the morning. Sometimes, that can be a heroic effort. Just remember: even the smallest step means you are hailing that taxi.

The applause you heard, just now, was for YOU!

*　　*　　*

Epilogue

Leaving Adversity Plaza

As I leave Cinnamon City, I feel refreshed, renewed, ready to deal with whatever happens in my life. I have gained much from visiting Adversity Plaza. No longer will I fear this place; I can see that even in the darkness, there is light.

I walk to the curb, raising my arm to hail the taxi. As the driver approaches, I step forward, confidently, holding my hand out with a smile. The driver hands me the keys, and disappears. I take the wheel and drive away from Adversity Plaza, into my future. I don't know what will happen next in my life, but I know who has the keys.

* * *

Leaving Adversity Plaza

Leaving behind the dark city, the dim plaza,
A place of constraints and worries,
A place of guilt and duties,
I come upon a yellow-green meadow,
A place bright with hope and velvet surprises.
I run forward, into the sun-dappled world ahead,
Streams and valleys, forests and mountains,
A world alight with love, hope, peace.
I am free, like a horse released from the reins.
I have made my choice. It is joy. I am home.

*   *   *